# More Advance Praise for *Happiness Is Free*

"In his great book, *Happiness Is Free, and It's Easier Than You Think*\*, Hale Dwoskin continues the lifelong work and teachings of the great Lester Levenson, and has written a 'do-it-yourself', 'easier than you think,' Method that has transformed lives worldwide! With the information and exercises learned from this book, you will be able to let go of all that keeps you from living a life free from all limitations and live a life of happiness, joy and peace."

**Diana Nightingale, Owner, Keys Publishing, Inc., international speaker, and author of *Learning To Fly As A Nightingale***

"*Happiness is Free* presents a psycho-spiritual perspective that applies the most esoteric wisdom to everyday human misery–and in a way that feels both practical and stunning, shows us how to move beyond insight and actually release what ails us. I am very grateful."

**Nancy Dreyfus, Psy.D. author of *Talk To Me Like I'm Someone You Love: FlashCards for Real Life.***

"Stop Striving!! Learn to 'Let it Happen', not 'Make it Happen.' Hale and Lester, two 'master teachers' teach you a truly effortless way to a great life through the simple principles outlined in *Happiness Is Free*. These simple techniques can change your life–FOREVER! What we learned in a four-day class in 1991 has been concisely synthesized in this wonderful, instructional book. You will actually discover how to stop being your own strongest barrier to success. Within months of learning Lester's principles we began to reach personal, professional, and spiritual heights we had never known existed. We heartily recommend that you learn it for yourself. Because Happiness IS Free, and it really IS easier than you think."

**Barbara Mark & Trudy Griswold, authors of *Angelspeake Trilogy and Heaven & Beyond: Conversations with Souls in Transition***

"In these times of turmoil and uncertainty, the simple yet profound truths expressed by Lester Levenson provide a powerful backdrop against which the events of our lives and our world can be seen and understood from an expanded perspective, bringing clarity and peacefulness in its wake. The commentaries provided by Hale Dwoskin help to build a bridge between the understanding of Lester's words and the organic integration of his wisdom into the day-to-day activities of our daily lives. For those already familiar with Lester's thoughts and with releasing, these volumes will bring additional depth and clarity to their understanding and practice. For those unfamiliar with Lester or his work, these volumes have the potential to be the doorway to a new way of looking at the world."

**Elliott Grumer, Psychiatrist, Phoenix, AZ**

\*Advance Praise For *Happiness Is Free* Book One

# Happiness Is Free

## ... and it's easier than you think!

# Book 5

*by* **Hale Dwoskin**
*&* **Lester Levenson**

**Sedona**
*Training Associates*

Printed in the U.S.A. by Malloy Inc. on acid free 85% recycled paper.

Publisher:

**Sedona Training Associates**

60 Tortilla Drive, Suite 2

Sedona, AZ 86336

Phone: (928) 282-3522

Fax: (928) 203-0602

E-mail: release@sedona.com

Web: www.sedona.com

Cover design and illustration by Lightbourne © 2001

Interior book design by Wendy Barratt

Library of Congress Number:

ISBN 0-915721-04-X

Set of 5 books ISBN 0-915721-05-8

Special pre-publication limited edition.

To all seekers and finders

of the ultimate happiness everywhere

and Sedona Method® graduates

worldwide

# Acknowledgments

I would like to thank the following people for making this book possible: My loving wife, Amy Edwards, all Sedona Method® graduates worldwide, Stephanie Gunning, Sara Whitcomb, Diane Brace, as well as all of the Sedona Training Associates staff.

# Table of Contents

Lester Levenson

# Happiness Is Free

*... and it's easier than you think!*

## Book 5

# Publisher's Note

If you have read any of the other books in this series, you will probably notice that the Introduction and How to Gain the Maximum Benefit from This Book sections are the same in each volume. This is done intentionally so that you can review them with each reading. If you have already read these chapters several times, you can choose to skip directly to the first session when exploring this book.

The Next Steps and Guidelines for *Happiness Is Free* Support Groups are also repeats. They are provided in this book for your convenient reference.

# Introduction

## What Is Happiness?

Quite simply put, happiness is you being your Self. Not the limited self that you pretend to be most of the time, but the unlimited Self that you are and have always been. This is the Self that is always effortlessly present before, during, and after everything else that appears in your experience. You are the radiant yet changeless background that allows for everything else to exist.

If that is true, you may be wondering, why is it so hard to discover and why have there been so many books written on the topic—including this one? The answer to that is not as simple.

We have spent eons pretending to be anything but unlimited. In fact, we have become so good at this pretending to be limited that we have forgotten that it is just a game, a pretense. We now spend most of our time bolstering the illusion that we have created for ourselves, leaving very little time for the inner reflection that can set us free from this totally self-imposed and artificial sense of limitation.

It takes tremendous energy to maintain the illusion that

unlimited Beingness is actually limited to the particular body-mind that you call yourself. No wonder we are so exhausted most of the time. We have unlimited energy available to us, but instead of using this energy for good or to discover who we truly are, we use this energy to convince ourselves and others around us that we are limited–that we have personal problems.

The late Lester Levenson, my friend and the coauthor of this book, used to say that extraditing ourselves from this situation in which we all find ourselves is either "simple or impossible." It is simple when we allow it to be easy. We can allow our energy to flow inwards towards self-discovery and for loving acceptance of what is. It is impossible when we force our energy to flow outwards. We fight against the world of our own creation and try to prove to everyone, including ourselves, that our world and its problems are real.

Are you ready to make it simple? You probably are if you were attracted to read this book. This book is designed to guide you experientially to rediscover your ultimate happiness by uncovering the real unlimited you.

The happiness that is you is totally independent of what you have or do not have, yet it improves your experience of whatever you have or don't have. This happiness that is you is also independent of what you do or do not do, yet it makes your experience of whatever you do or don't do more enjoyable. This happiness really is who you are, and you can experience it for yourself by reading this book and following the simple suggestions contained within it.

I know that you have probably heard promises like these before. And you may have often been disappointed. Which, of course, could make you a little skeptical. If you are in doubt, that is okay. I encourage you to believe nothing that you read in this book until you can prove it for yourself. But I promise you that this program is different. I have the absolute conviction that you can uncover your ultimate happiness and live it in every moment. This conviction is based on my own direct experience over the last quarter century of working with Lester Levenson and his teachings and then sharing them with thousands of people around the world.

Yet I did not always feel convinced. I met Lester Levenson in 1976. Back then I was an ardent, although confused seeker who had gone to many trainings and seminars led by teachers from both the East and the West. I had studied various body-centered disciplines, including Yoga, Tai Chi, and Shiatsu. I had actively participated in various courses, including EST, Actualism, Theta Seminars, and Rebirthing. I had many nice experiences at these seminars, and heard and understood–at least intellectually–many useful concepts. Still I felt incomplete. I longed for a simple and powerful answer to some important, yet vexing questions like: "What is my life's purpose?" "What is truth?" and "Who am I?"

Much of what I had heard and experienced only added to my questioning. No one seemed to have truly satisfying answers or have truly satisfied him or herself about what their true nature was or what was the ultimate truth. There was also a strong, almost universal belief that growing was hard work and required baring your soul and reliving painful, unresolved issues. However, that all changed during a very fortunate encounter with a remarkable man.

I met Lester at a seminar that I had organized for a well-known speaker, which Lester attended as the seminar leader's guest. That day, a group of us went out to lunch together, where Lester's presence immediately struck me as special. He was in total peace and equal-mindedness, very comfortable with himself. He was unassuming and easy to talk to, and treated everyone as his friend—even me, a complete stranger. It was obvious that he had ended his search by discovering the answers I'd been seeking. I knew I had to find out more.

When I asked Lester what he did, he invited me to a seminar that was being held the next weekend. All he would tell me about it was that, "a group of people is going to sit around a table and release." I wasn't sure what that meant, but I knew if it could even point me in the direction of the qualities of which Lester was the living embodiment, I definitely wanted it. I took a leap of faith and signed up on the spot.

Almost overnight I knew that I had found what I was looking for. In fact, deep inside I knew that this process of releasing and Lester's teachings were what I had been born to do and share with the world—and to this day I have never wavered.

Before we move on to explore more of what you can expect from this book, I would like to share Lester's story with you in his own words. The quote that follows is very similar to the story that Lester unfolded for me shortly after I met him and started exploring his teachings:

I was born July 19, 1909, in Elizabeth, New Jersey, into a middle class family as a very shy person. I tried to do things the way they were supposed to be done—doing the right thing, getting a good education, and being the best in my field. My natural inclination was towards science, especially the science of the world, and of man himself. I graduated from Rutgers University in 1931 as a physicist, after which I worked twenty-some years in physics and engineering.

In physics, I worked in research and development on measuring instruments and automatic control, connected with Brown Instrument Co., which later became a subsidiary of Honeywell. And in the engineering field, I worked as a mechanical engineer, an electrical engineer, a construction engineer, a heating and venting engineer, and a marine engineer—actually, fourteen different fields.

I also went into various businesses, including restaurants, lumber, building, and oil, intertwined with engineering, wanting to make money, wanting to make it in the world. At that time, I did not know what I now know—that what I was seeking was actually the answers to life itself. Nothing that I had worked at would give me that answer, and as the years went by, I became heavy with depression and with sickness.

By 1952, I had been through constant illness—I even had jaundice three or so times a year. I had an enlarged liver, kidney stones, spleen trouble, hyper- and hypo-acidity, ulcers that perforated and formed lesions, and to top it off, I had at least ten years of migraine headaches. This all culminated in 1952 when I had my second coronary thrombosis.

After the second coronary, I was told I would not live much longer—that I might die any day and shouldn't make the effort to take so much as a step unless I necessarily had to. I was extremely fearful of dying, but I said to myself, "You're still breathing, Lester—there is still a chance." So I sat down and began thinking on an "around the clock" basis. Having lived forty-two or so years, and having reached the end of the line without happiness, without health, I realized that all the knowledge I had accumulated was of no avail. I had studied Watson's behaviorism in the 30's and Freud's in the late 30's and early 40's. I had studied the philosophies. I had studied logic. I studied economics. I studied all the major fields of man, and with all that knowledge there, I was at the end of the line. This made me realize that the accumulated knowledge of man was of no use.

So I decided to start from scratch. Forget all that knowledge. Begin from point zero and see what you can pick up. So, I posed the questions, "What am I?" "What is this World?" "What is my relationship to it?" "What is Mind?" "What is Intelligence?" "What is Happiness?"

I began by asking myself, "What do I want out of life?" And the answer was happiness. Investigating further, I went into the moment when I was feeling happiest. I discovered something which to me was startling at the time. It was when I was loving that I was happiest. That happiness equated to my capacity to love rather than to being loved. That was a starting point.

I began correcting all my thoughts and feelings in that direction from that of wanting to be loved, to that of loving. And in that process, I discovered another major thing that kind of shocked me. I saw that I wanted to change this entire world, and that was the cause of my ulcers—or one of the major causes. In realizing how much I wanted to change things in this world, I saw how it made me a slave of this world, I made the decision to reverse that. And in the process of following out these two directions—actually unloading all the subconscious concepts and pressures in those directions—I discovered I was getting happier, freer, lighter, and feeling better in general.

As I saw this direction was good, I made the decision that if a slice of pie tasted this good, I wanted the whole pie. And I decided not to let go of this direction until I got that entire pie of happiness, and with it the answer to, "What am I? What is this life, and what is my relationship to it?" This decision allowed me, as I claim, to get the answer to life itself in a matter of only three months. I believe if I can do it, anyone can do it if they have that much "want to."

In that three-month period, all the ailments I had in my physical body corrected. All my miseries dropped away. And I ended up in a place in which I was happy all the time, without sorrow. Not that the world stopped pushing against me, it continued–but I was at a place where I could resolve things almost immediately. Having cleared out the negative fears, all the negative "I cannots," I would focus right on the answer to every problem, and get it very quickly. And so, my whole life turned around from being depressed and sick, to being happy all the time, and being in perfect health all the time.

One of the things that happened in this process was my identification with others. I saw that we are all related, we are all interconnected, each mind is like a radio broadcasting and receiving station; that we are all tuned into each other unconsciously–that we are just not aware of it. As a lot of the suppressed energies are let out, this becomes obvious to us and once we identify with everyone else it is just natural that we want everyone else to discover what we have discovered. That life was meant to be beautiful... meant to be happy all the time with no sorrow. And to be with perfect health. And so after reaching that high point of understanding in 1952, I have wanted to help others to discover what I had discovered.

I was deeply moved by Lester's story because it offered hope for all of us who may not have had the good fortune to have an ideal life. Lester was able to discover his true nature in a relatively short time and despite extreme adversity. If he could do it, I knew that I could, too.

The following quote is Lester expanding more about his actual realization:

I was at the end of my rope. I was told not to take a step unless I absolutely had to because there was a possibility that I could drop dead at any moment.

This was a terrible, shocking thing, suddenly to be told that I couldn't be active anymore, having been so active all my life. It was a horrible thing. An intense fear of dying overwhelmed me, the fear that I might drop dead any minute. This stayed with me for days. I went through a real, horrible, low, spinning period there, in the grip of intense fear of dying or of being a cripple for the rest of my life in that I wouldn't be able to be active. I felt that life would not be worthwhile any more.

This caused me to conclude with determination, "Either I get the answers, or I'll take me off this earth. No heart attack will do it!" I had a nice easy way to do it, too. I had morphine the doctors gave me for my kidney stone attacks.

After several days of this intense fear of dying, I suddenly realized, "Well, I'm still alive. As long as I'm alive there's hope. As long as I'm alive, maybe I can get out of this. What do I do?"

Well, I was always a smart boy, always made the honor roll. Even got myself a four-year scholarship to Rutgers University at a time when scholarships were very rare through competitive examinations. But what does this avail me? Nothing! Here I am with all this brilliance, as miserable and scared as can be.

Then I said, "Lester, you were not only not smart, you were

Dumb! Dumb! Dumb! There's something wrong in your intellect. With all your knowledge, you've come to this bottom end! Drop all this knowledge you've so studiously picked up on philosophy, psychology, social science, and economics! It is of no avail! Start from scratch. Begin all over again your search for the answers.

And with an extreme desperation and intense wanting out–not wanting to die, I began to question, "What am I? What is this world? What is my relationship to it? What do I want from it?"

"Happiness."

"Well, what is happiness?"

"Being loved."

"But I am loved. I know several very desirable girls with beauty, charm, and intellect who want me. And I have the esteem of my friends. Yet, I'm miserable!"

I sensed that the closest thing related to happiness was love. So I began reviewing and reliving my past love affairs, looking at the points where the little happiness that I had were. I began to pull up and dissect all my high moments of loving. Suddenly, I got an inkling that it was when I was loving that I had the highest feeling!

I remembered one evening, a beautiful balmy evening in the mountains when I was camping with my girlfriend. We were both lying on the grass, both looking up at the sky, and I had my arm around her. The nirvana, the perfection of the height of happiness was right there. I was feeling how great is love for my girlfriend! How wonderful is knowing all this nature! How perfect a setting!

Then I saw that it was my loving her that was the cause of this happiness! Not the beauty of the setting or being with my girlfriend.

Then I immediately turned to the other side. Boy it was great when she loved me! I remembered the moment when publicly this beautiful, charming girl told the world that she approved of Lester, she loved Lester–and I could feel that nice feeling of approval. But I sensed that it was not as great as what I had just discovered. It was not a lasting feeling. It was just for the moment. In order for me to have that feeling continuously, she had to continue saying that.

So, this momentary ego approval was not as great as the feeling of loving her! As long as I was loving her, I felt so happy. But when she loved me, there were only moments of happiness when she gave me approval.

Days of further cogitation gradually revealed to me that this was correct! I was happier when I loved her than I was when I got that momentary ego-satisfaction when she loved me. Her loving me was a momentary pleasure that needed constant showing and proving on her part, while my loving her was a constant happiness, as long as I was loving her.

I concluded that my happiness equated to my loving! If I could increase my loving, then I could increase my happiness! This was the first inkling I had as to what brings about happiness. And it was a tremendous thing because I hadn't had happiness. And I said, "Gee, if this is the key to happiness, I've got the greatest!" Even the hope of getting more and more happiness was a tremendous thing, because this was the number one thing I wanted–happiness.

That started me on weeks and weeks of reviewing my past love affairs. I dug up from the past, incident after incident when I thought I was loving, and I discovered that I was being nice to my girlfriends, trying to get them to love me, and that that was selfish. That was not really love. That was just wanting my ego bolstered!

I kept reviewing incidents from the past, and where I saw that I was not loving, I would change that feeling to loving that person.

Instead of wanting them to do something for me, I would change it to my wanting to do something for them. I kept this up until I couldn't find any more incidents to work on.

This insight on love, seeing that happiness was determined by my capacity to love, was a tremendous insight. It began to free me, and any bit of freedom when you're plagued feels so good. I knew that I was in the right direction. I had gotten hold of a link of the chain of happiness and was determined not to let go until I had the entire chain.

I felt a greater freedom. There was an easier concentration of my mind because of it. And I began to look better at my mind. What is my mind? What is intelligence?

Suddenly, a picture flashed of amusement park bumper-cars that are difficult to steer so that they continually bump into each other. They all get their electrical energy from the wire screen above the cars through a pole coming down to every car.

The power above was symbolic of the overall intelligence and energy of the universe coming down the pole to me and everyone else, and to the degree we step on the gas do we use it. Each driver of the cars is taking the amount of energy and intelligence that he wants from that wire, but he steers his car blindly and bumps into other cars, and bumps and bumps.

I saw that if I chose to, I could take more and more of that overall intelligence.

And so I dug into that. I began to examine thinking and its relationship to what was happening. And it was revealed that everything that was happening had a prior thought behind it and that I never before related the thought and the happening because of the element of time between the two.

When I saw that everything that was happening to me had a thought of it before it happened, I realized that if I could grab hold of this, I could consciously determine everything that was happening to me!

And above all, I saw that I was responsible for everything that had happened to me, formerly thinking that the world was abusing me! I saw that my whole past life, and all that tremendous effort to make money and in the end, failing, was due only to my thinking!

This was a tremendous piece of freedom, to think that I was not a victim of this world, that it lay within my power to arrange the world the way I wanted it to be, that rather than being an effect of it, I could now be at cause over it and arrange it the way I would like it to be!

That was a tremendous realization, a tremendous feeling of freedom!

I was so ill when I started my searching; I had one foot in the grave. And when I saw that my thinking was cause for what was happening to me, I immediately saw my body from my chin down to my toes as perfect. And instantly, I knew it was perfect! I knew the lesions and adhesions of my intestine due to perforated ulcers were undone. I knew everything within me was in perfect running order.

And it was.

Discovering that my happiness equated to my loving, discovering that my thinking was the cause of things happening to me in my life gave me more and more freedom. Freedom from unconscious compulsions that I had to work, I had to make money, and I had to have girls. Freedom in the feeling that I was now able to determine my destiny, I was now able to control my world, I was now able to arrange my environment to suit me. This new freedom lightened my internal burden so greatly that I felt that I had no need to do anything.

Plus, the new happiness I was experiencing was so great! I was experiencing a joy that I had never known existed. I had never dreamed happiness could be so great.

I determined "If this is so great, I'm not going to let go of it until I carry it all the way!" I had no idea how joyous a person could be.

So, I began digging further on how to extend this joy. I began further changing my attitudes on love. I would imagine the girl I wanted most marrying one of my friends, or the boy I would want her to marry least, and then enjoy their enjoying each other. To me, this was the extreme in loving, and if I could achieve it, it would give me more of this wonderful thing that I was experiencing.

And so I worked on it. I took a particular fellow, Burl, and a particular girl, and I wouldn't let go until I could really feel the joy of their enjoying each other.

Then I knew I had it–or almost had it.

Then later on, I had further tests of this in talking to people who were opposing me no end when I was trying to help them. I would consciously feel the greatest love for them when they were attacking me. And the joy of loving them was so wonderful, I would, without any thought, thank them so profusely for having given me the opportunity of talking with them, that it threw them into a dither.

But I really felt that. I thanked them from the bottom of my heart for having given me the opportunity of loving them when they were making it as difficult as they possibly could. I didn't express that to them. I just thanked them for the opportunity of having been able to talk with them.

That I was able to do this was good news to me because, like other things, I was able to carry loving to the extreme. I could love people who were opposing me.

And I would not stop until I could see the end of the line of this happiness I was getting. I would go higher and higher and higher and say, "Oh, my gosh, there can be nothing higher than this!" But I would try. And, I would go higher. Then I would say, "Oh, there can't be anything higher than this!" But I would try, and go higher! And then say, "Oh, there can't be anything happier than this!" until I realized there was no limit to happiness!

I would get incapacitated. I could look at my body, and I couldn't move it I was so top-heavy with ecstasy and joy. I was actually incapacitated. I would do this for hours, going higher and higher and then I would have to work for hours to keep coming down and down and down until I could start being the body again in order to operate it.

Contemplating the source of intelligence and energy, I discovered that energy, as well as intelligence was available in unlimited amounts, and that it came simply by my freeing myself from all compulsions, inhibitions, entanglements, hang-ups. I saw that I had dammed up this energy, this power, and all I had to do was pry loose the logs of the dam which were my compulsions and hang-ups–and that was what I did. As I let go of these things, I was removing logs and allowing this infinite energy to flow, just like a water dam flows if you pull the logs out, one by one. The more logs you pull out, the greater the flow. All I needed to do was to remove these logs and let the infinite power and energy flow.

Seeing this, the power that was right behind my mind was allowed to flow through like it had never flowed before. There were times when I'd get this realization of what I am that would put so much energy into me, I would just jump up in the air from my chair. I would go right straight out the front door, and I would start walking and walking and walking, for hours at a time–sometimes for days at a time! I just felt as though my body would not contain it, that I had to walk or run some of it off. I remember walking the streets of New York City in the wee hours of the morning, just walking at a very good pace, and not being able to do anything otherwise! I had to expend some of that energy. It was so tremendous.

I saw that the source of all this energy, of all intelligence was basically harmonious, and that harmony was the rule of the universe. And that was why the planets were not colliding, and that was why the sun rose every day, and that was why everything functioned.

When I started my search, I was a very convinced and absolute materialist. The only thing that was real was that which you could feel and touch. My understanding of the world was as solid as concrete. And when some of these revelations came to me that the world was just a result of my mind, that thinking determined all matter, that matter had no intelligence, and that our intelligence determined all matter and everything about it. When I saw that the solidity that I formerly had was only a thought itself, my nice, solid, concrete foundations began to crack. Twenty years of buildup began to tumble.

And my body shook, and shook so much; I just shook for days. I shook just like a nervous old person. I knew that the concrete view I had had of the world was never going to be again. But it didn't drop away gracefully, with ease. For days, I actually shook, until I think I shook the whole thing loose.

Then, my view was just the opposite of what it had been

months previously, that the real solid thing was not the physical world, was not my mind, but something, that was much greater. The very essence, the very Beingness of me was the reality. It had no limits, it was eternal, and all the things that I saw before were the least of me, rather than the all of me. The all of me was by Beingness.

I saw that the only limitations I had were the ones that I accepted. So, wanting to know what am I? And looking for this unlimited Being that I had had an inkling of, I got insight of this tremendous unlimited Being that I am.

And on seeing that, I right there and then realized, "Well, I'm not this limited body and I thought I was! I am not this mind with its limitations that I thought I was!"

And I undid all body limitation, and almost all mind limitation, just by saying, "I am not it! Finished! Done! Period! That's it!" I so declared.

It was obvious to me that I wasn't that body and mind that I had thought I was. I just saw that's all! It's simple when you see it.

I let go of identifying with this body. And when I did that, I saw that my Beingness was all Beingness. That Beingness is like one grand ocean. It's not chopped up into parts called drops of bodies. It's all one ocean.

This caused me to identify with every being, every person and even every atom in this universe. Then you are finished forever with separation and all the hellishness that's caused only by separation.

Then you can no more be fooled by the apparent limitations of the world. You see them as a dream, as an appearancy, because you know that your very own Beingness has no limits.

In reality, the only thing that is, is Beingness. That is the real, changeless substance behind everything.

Everything of life itself was open to me, the total understanding of it. It is simply that we are infinite beings, over which we have superimposed concepts of limitation (the logs of the dam). And we are smarting under these limitations that we accept for ourselves as though they are real, because they are opposed to our basic nature of total freedom.

Life before and after my realization was at two different extremes. Before, it was just extreme depression, intense misery, and sickness. After, it was a happiness and serenity that's indescribable. Life became so beautiful and so harmonious that all day, every day, everything would fall perfectly into line.

As I would drive through New York City, I would rarely hit a red light. When I would go to park my car, people, sometimes two or three people, would stop and even step into the street to help direct me into a parking space. There were times when taxi cab drivers would see me looking for a parking space and would give up their space for me. And after they did, they couldn't understand why they had done it. There they were, double-parked!

Even policemen who were parked would move out and give me their parking place. And again, after they did, they couldn't understand why. But I knew they felt good in doing so. And they would continue to help me.

If I went into a store, the salesman would happily go out of his way to help me. Or, if I would order something in a restaurant and then change my mind, the waitress would bring what I wanted, even though I hadn't told her.

Actually everyone moves to serve you as you just float around. When you are in tune and you have a thought, every atom in the universe moves to fulfill your thought. And this is true.

Being in harmony is such a delightful, delectable state, not because things are coming your way, but because of the feeling of God-in-operation. It's a tremendous feeling; you just can't imagine how great it is. It is such a delight when you're in tune, in harmony–you see God everywhere! You're watching God in operation. And that is what you enjoy, rather than the time, the incident, the happening. His operation is the ultimate.

When we get in tune, our capacity to love is so extreme that we love everyone with an extreme intensity that makes living the most delightful it could ever be.


When I found the quote above I was deeply moved, and as I worked to put this book together I knew it was important for you to be exposed to it as well so you could appreciate the point of view from which Lester did his teaching.

Lester dedicated the rest of his life, from 1952 through his death in 1994, as he put it, to "helping the rest of him discover what he had discovered." He joyously lived for others without any sense of sacrifice, tirelessly working to help them to discover their true nature or at least let go of their suffering. Despite his best intentions he was not always understood. He used to say, "You only hear ten percent of what I say." Which, in my experience working with him and watching how others related to him, was quite generous. In fact, the very people that he helped the most often vehemently opposed him. But this never deterred him, nor did it ever shake his unqualified happiness and peace.

He worked with people on a one-to-one basis and in small groups, teaching sessions very much like those you will experience in this book. Until, around 1974, with the help of some of his closest students, he summarized his teaching into a do-it-yourself system that we now call the Sedona Method®. He did this to take himself out of the teaching loop. No matter how often he protested to the contrary, his students would often attribute their gains and realizations to him because they felt so elevated in his presence. He wanted everyone to know that they could discover just what he had on their own without needing an external teacher.

As you read this book and work with the material contained with in it, you will have a direct experience of Lester's teaching style through his words and their import. This is significant because it is something that very few people were lucky enough to experience during the last twenty years of his life. You will also have the benefit of seeing how his teachings have evolved since the creation of the Sedona Method® and in the work of his students since his passing.

Before Lester died, he asked me to continue his work and to continue to find ways to make the experience of letting go more readily available to those who are interested. That is why I have added some commentary and suggestions at the end of each session. I hope you will find these as helpful as I did.

I urge you to treat this book as a home study course in discovering your true nature and uncovering your innate happiness. You can benefit from this book even if you only read it casually. But if you dedicate yourself to using it to the fullest, the results you can achieve will astound you.

# How to Gain the Maximum Benefit
# from This Book

A Seven-week Course on Liberating the
Happiness, Peace, and Joy Within

This book is designed to be a seven-week home study course on the ultimate happiness. Read and work with one chapter per week. Each chapter contains a session from Lester along with my comments and suggestions to help you understand his message, as well as space for note and realizations. However, I would suggest that you do your best to get the most out of Lester's words in each session before moving on to the commentary. You may need to allow some extra time to sit with each paragraph or the whole session. You may also want to revisit the chapter repeatedly throughout the week.

You Have All the Time in the World

We live in an incredibly fast paced world where we are constantly forcing ourselves to move more rapidly in order just to keep up. In our rush to attain our goals, especially in the spiritual realm, we are often rushing past the very moment that offers the greatest opportunity for self-recognition–now. If you read this book in a hurry you may find you get what Lester used to call "spiritual indigestion." Therefore, I highly encourage you to read this material and approach it as an exploration of life as though you have all the time in the world.

## Don't Believe Anything We Say

Especially with spiritual teachers, there is a tendency simply to accept what they say on hearsay or belief. Lester strongly felt that we should avoid doing this with any teacher. Instead we should allow ourselves to stay open to a teacher's message as an exploration or an experiment in consciousness. We should only accept what he or she teaches once we can prove it for ourselves through our own experience. Lester used to call this "taking it for checking."

I suggest that you take everything that you are exposed to in this book for checking. Allow yourself to be as open to the message as you can without accepting it on blind faith. You will find that this material has much more value for you when you explore it in your own life.

On the other hand, I also highly recommend that you suspend comparison and judgment as best you can. You may find that some of what you are exposed to in this book contradicts what you have learned from other teachers. I would suggest that you do not throw out the other material that you have learned, but merely put it aside as best you can while you explore these sessions. Once you have had time to draw your own conclusions, then you can go back and compare this material to everything else you have learned and see where it fits.

Contradiction is inevitable when you compare different paths or traditions of growth. However, this does not invalidate the different points of view. What every good teacher does is speak to the audience at hand to the best of their ability. Sometimes they may appear to contradict themselves because each audience they address needs to experience the teachings from different levels or perspectives. For this reason you may even notice apparent contradictions between me and Lester and Lester and himself. Contradiction can be most palpable when you compare different teachers. Not only are they speaking to different audiences, they are also bringing their own unique perspective to the topic—as they should be.

When it comes to truth, if you can allow yourself to embrace all possibilities you will find yourself understanding and applying the wisdom you gain on a much more useful, deeper, and heartfelt level. There are many rays that lead to the one sun.

## It Is a Matter of Resonance

From my perspective, everything in the world has its own vibration or resonance, including you and everyone you meet. Have you ever noticed that some people tend to pull you up when you are with them and others seem to pull you down, and that they often don't need to say or do anything to have this effect on you? As we grow in understanding on the path, our resonance or frequency tends to go up. But it is not just a matter of higher or lower. We all relate better with some people than others, even if they are on the same level of vibration as us. Of course the same thing is true for teachers.

As you read this material, you may find that you resonate intensely with certain statements while others leave you feeling blank or unmoved. Lester recommended that you highlight the chapters, phrases, or statements that move you most for future reference, then go back and spend some time pondering them. Over time, as you revisit this material, other parts of it will stand out more than they did initially. That is because you will have changed and become ready to see things from a new perspective. When this happens, allow yourself to honor the change and shift your focus accordingly.

## About Lester's Language

Lester had a unique way of using the English language. I have purposely preserved his style of communication because I've noticed that when you read or listen to any teacher in his or her own vernacular, the words have more of an import than when they have been heavily edited. My intention here is to give you the feel of having been present as Lester's talks unfolded, so that you can be as open as possible to his deepest message.

Lester came to this unique communication style for several reasons. His realization came quickly and spontaneously without him following any particular teacher or discipline or even having done any reading or studying of the path. Thus he had no language that adequately expressed what he was experiencing and what he wanted to share with others. As a result he looked in existing spiritual books from both the East and the West to try and find a suitable language that would best communicate his amazing discoveries. From the East, he was attracted to the teachings and writings of Ramana Maharshi and Paramahansa Yogananda. From the West, he drew upon the Bible, especially the New Testament. You will probably notice the influence of these sources in his writing. Occasionally he even slips into old English to express himself.

Most of the Lester material in this book comes from talks that took place in the 1960's and early 1970's. Therefore he often uses a vernacular that was more appropriate for that era. You will notice that his reference to current events and things like population figures are also reflective of that same time period.

In addition, Lester had difficulty grounding himself in time. He saw time as a self-imposed limitation or merely a concept. He would refer to things as happening yesterday that happened ten or twenty years earlier, and things that were about to happen that have yet to occur. He always seemed to be factually accurate and yet frequently was not able to place his perceptions in the appropriate time period.

Lester also did not believe in the limitation of space, so here and there often had the same meaning to him. He would often refer to getting "there" when referring to Beingness when he really meant "here." Or "going free" when he knew there was nowhere to go. He also used language this way because he was wanting to communicate to people where they were. Most people believe that Beingness is apart from where they are now. That's why they go looking for it. The "there" that Lester referred to when speaking of Beingness is closer than your breath.

Lester also learned his instructing style from an old school that uses imperatives heavily. He often used the charged words "should," "have to," "must," and "only." These charged words were often used by Lester to wake people up by using a little extra force. If you notice that these words stir up resistance in you, this in normal. These words tend to do that in most of us. Allow yourself to let go of the resistance as best you can and be open to the underlying message.

Please keep these points in mind as you read the sessions so you can allow yourself to remain as open as possible to his message without getting lost in how it is being communicated.

## When Two or More Are Gathered in Thy Name

The exercises that follow each session have been or will be explored as part of the advanced courses we teach at Sedona Training Associates. They are designed so that you can benefit from either doing them on your own or sharing them with a friend, relative, or loved one. There is an awesome power that is unleashed when we gather together to focus on truth. That is why Sedona Training Associates hosts live seminars to explore this topic and why you can benefit from sharing this material with others.

If you choose to do the exercises at the end of each session with someone else, you can ask each other the questions or lead each other in the explorations. All you need to do is be as present as you can with your partner and ask them the questions in the third person using the pronoun "you" instead of "I." Grant your partner their Beingness by allowing them to have their own exploration.

When you are asking your partner to let go, do your best to let go as you facilitate your partner in releasing. You will find that this happens naturally if you are open to it. Refrain from leading, judging their responses, or giving them advice. Also refrain from discussing the explorations until you have both completed them during that sitting and you mutually agree to discuss them. Also validate your partner's point of view even if it does not agree with your own.

Please refrain from playing the role of counselor or therapist unless you're a trained counselor or therapist and have been specifically asked by your partner to play this role with them. Also, if they bring up a medical condition that would ordinarily require a trained medical professional, suggest that they get whatever support they need in this area. If you are not sure whether or not they truly need medical support, you can suggest it anyhow, just to be sure.

## Write Down Your Gains

As you move diligently through this material, you will find that it has many powerful positive effects on you. We call the changes that come from this exploration "gains," and I highly recommend that you write them down, as they occur, to spur you on to even greater self-discovery.

The following is a list of some gains you can expect as you work with this book:

- Positive changes in behavior and/or attitude
- Greater ease, effectiveness, and joy in daily activities
- More open and effective communications
- Increased problem solving ability
- Greater flexibility
- More relaxed and confident in action
- Accomplishments
- Completions
- New beginnings
- Acquiring new abilities or skills
- Increase in positive feelings
- Decrease in negative feelings
- More love towards all beings

As you read and explore this material you will also have realizations about your own patterns of limitation and realizations about the nature of Reality itself. I highly recommend that you write these down as well.

There are seven blank pages at the end of each session, one for each day of the week, which are designed for you to write down your gains and realizations.

## Be Open to the Unexpected

Realizations and gains definitely will come as you consciously work with this material, however, they will also come when you least expect them. Often it is when we are not looking for, or trying to accomplish anything that the mind relaxes enough to allow realization. So make room for this possibility throughout your day. As best you can, relax and accept that the timing of your greatest breakthroughs and realizations, including the ultimate realization of your true nature, may be totally out of your control.

## It Is All a Matter of Letting Go or Releasing

Lester strongly believed that growing on the path was a function of your willingness, ability, and follow-through in letting go. He was so adamant about this point that he dedicated the last twenty years of his life solely to this one aspect of his teachings and encouraged the development and practice of what we now call the Sedona Method®. To get the most from this book, I highly recommend that you learn the Sedona Method® and practice it as you read and work with Lester's material. Even if you don't, I highly encourage you to do some form of letting go in order to deal with whatever this material invariably brings up into your consciousness.

You will get the most out of it if you allow yourself to let go as best you can.

To this end, I will be making suggestions throughout the book of what and how to let go as you explore what Lester has to offer. I have also included the following guidelines on releasing so that you can start to apply this technique in your life as you study this course in the ultimate happiness.

## Holistic Releasing™

Holistic Releasing™ is the latest advancement in the continuing improvement and development of the process that we at Sedona Training Associates call letting go, releasing, or the Sedona Method®. If you've worked with us before, you're aware that in our Sedona Method® classes and taped programs we mainly focus on three methods of letting go. The first is letting go by choosing or making a decision just to drop whatever we're holding onto in the present moment. The second is letting go by allowing whatever is to be in this moment, welcoming it fully and seeing it almost like the clouds that pass through the sky, needing no correction, no changing, no fixing. The third way is letting go by diving into the very core of whatever the feeling is. When we dive into the very core of any feeling, we discover that it's empty inside—or full of goodness—not full of the darkness that we generally assume will be there.

I recently developed a fourth way of letting go that we call Holistic Releasing™. This process is what many of the suggestions at the end of each chapter are all about. It has two purposes. If you've worked with the Sedona Method® before, it's a way of deepening the work that you're already doing. And if you haven't worked with the Sedona Method® before, it's a way to open your understanding of the whole process of letting go. It is a way of having whatever you want in life.

The Holistic Releasing™ process will help you to collapse, dissolve, or let go of whatever sense of inner limitation you may be experiencing in your life. As you work with the suggestions throughout this book, your understanding of this new process will deepen and you'll find yourself spontaneously practicing this process in life–noticing more possibilities and seeing alternatives. You will feel more flexible, more open, and much more capable of handling whatever life dishes out to you.

Holistic Releasing™ is based on the premise that everything we experience in life, whether real or imagined, arises in pairs or polarities or duality. Because of life's underlying unity, if we have "in," we also have "out." If we have "right," we also have "wrong." If we have "good," we also have "bad." If we have "pain," we also have "pleasure." This is quite obvious. However when we live life as though we can hold onto the good and get rid of the bad, we miss the inner truth. When we try to hold onto something good, it always slips away. Whenever we try to clutch onto what we judge as good or preferable, it tends to move through our awareness.

Then think about the converse. What happens when we resist or try to hold away what we don't like? That is right. It persists or gets even bigger. So in effect what we've been doing is pulling what we don't like towards us and pushing what we do like away. We also spend a lot of time and energy magnifying the polarity by trying to keep what we like as far away as possible from what we don't like. All of this is creating the exact opposite effect of what we want: magnifying or even creating what we call problems.

I have discovered that when you bring the two sides of a

polarity together, it's like bringing matter and antimatter together, or positive and negative energy. The pair neutralizes each other and you're left with much greater freedom, greater presence, and greater understanding. You see solutions, not problems. You feel more open, more alive, and more at peace. As you work with the material in this book, you'll discover that this effect magnifies over time. You will start to discover more possibilities and see things more clearly. Every time you work with any of the suggestions in this book, you'll get more out of them—more inner understanding.

Now, the way we do this is very simple. We simply focus on both sides of the polarity by going back and forth. For instance, a very simple polarity has to do with happiness. Most of us are either feeling relatively happy or unhappy from moment to moment, and we see only one, not the other. So let's just do a little experiment. Could you allow yourself to feel as unhappy as you do in this moment? And then, could you allow yourself to feel as happy as you do in this moment? And as unhappy as you do in this moment? And as happy as you do in this moment? Do this a few more times and then notice how you feel inside.

To practice Holistic Releasing™, I suggest you continually go back and forth on each side of the particular polarity you are exploring. Do this several times in a row and you'll notice something happening inside. The polarities dissolve each other. You may have already noticed this just by doing the exercise. You are left with greater and greater freedom and presence. You may see the underlying unity beneath the apparent duality and separation of the polarities. You may also experience it as an energetic shift. You may feel it as a sense of dissolving or clearing or lightness. You may have greater clarity and understanding within your own self.

The way to get the most out of this process is merely to stay as open and as fully engaged as you can from moment to moment. As you ask the questions or repeat the statements to yourself, please do so with as open a mind and a heart as possible, doing your best not to lead with either one. If you must lead with one, do your best to lead with your heart–your feeling sense. Allow yourself to be as open as you can to the thoughts, feelings, sensations, and pictures that arise when you repeatedly ponder the statements or questions. Even better, try not to do anything except to stay open on every level. Let this process–releasing–do you.

The initial results from working with a polarity may be subtle. But as you work with it, the results will become more and more profound. And if you're persistent in working on any particular polarity, you'll reach a place of neutrality, or you'll reach a place of great expansion inside, as you've dissolved your sense of limitation.

You may reach a point where you feel as though you've had enough. If this does happen, you can either allow yourself to relax even more into the process or simply take a break. Do something to break the pattern of the moment. Go for a walk, stand up and stretch, open your eyes and look around the room, or close your eyes if you had them open. Then come back to working with yourself.

Do your best to start noticing how you create artificial polarities in life and begin to bring the two sides of these polarities together. Even in noticing them they will start to dissolve, leaving you with growing understanding and freedom. Please let yourself enjoy this work that we do together. Allow it to be fun and easy. Remember, growth can be fun!

**The following questions and answers will help you get the**

most from the process of releasing. In addition to reading them now, review them as often as needed as you work through the material in this book.

## How can I best do this process?

This process will help you to free yourself from all of your unwanted patterns of behavior, thought, and feeling. All that it requires from you is to be as open as you can to the process. It will free you to access clearer thinking, yet it is not a thinking process. It will help you to access heightened creativity, although you don't need to be particularly creative to be effective at doing this.

Sometimes we will use statements and sometimes we will use questions. When we use questions, we are merely asking you if it is possible to take this action. "Yes" or "No" are both acceptable answers. You will often let go even if you say, "No." As best you can, answer the question that you choose with a minimum of thought, staying away from second-guessing or getting into a debate with yourself about the merits of this action or its consequences. All the questions used in this process are deliberately simple. They are not important in and of themselves, but rather are designed to point you to the experience of letting go.

This process actually does itself. By simply switching back and forth in your mind between the two unique points of view that make up each polarity, they dissolve each other. As you work with this material, simply be as engaged as you can with an open mind and heart. Allow whatever thoughts, feelings, and limiting beliefs or pictures arise in your consciousness to just be there–welcome them as fully as you can. You do not even need to try and let them go. They will naturally dissolve each other.

### What are some of the ways I can apply this in my life?

Any time you find yourself being able to perceive only one possibility, either internally or externally, there is a high likelihood that you are missing at least one or more possibilities. Develop the habit of looking for alternatives and then doing the releasing process to gain more inner clarity.

If you find yourself judging yourself or others, you can simply allow yourself to switch back and forth between the judgment you have and its opposite. If you find yourself stuck in any way, allow yourself to be as stuck as you are and as unstuck as you are. Allow yourself to be creative as you work with this process, and you will find yourself seeing more and more possibilities and opening to having it all including the ultimate happiness.

The following is a list of generic questions that you can use to work on your own issues and polarities:

Could I allow myself to resist _____ as much as I do?
Could I allow myself to welcome (allow) _____ as best as I can?

Could I allow myself to reject _____ as much as I do?
Could I allow myself to accept _____ as best as I can?

Could I allow myself to dislike _____ as much as I do?
Could I allow myself to like _____ as much as I do?

Could I allow myself to hate _____ as much as I do?
Could I allow myself to love _____ as best as I can?

Could I allow myself to want to change _____ as much as I do?
Could I allow myself to let go of wanting to change _____ as best I can?

Could I allow myself to say no to _____ ?

Could I allow myself to say yes to _____ ?

Could I allow myself to be as open to _____ as I am?
Could I allow myself to be as closed to _____ as I am?

## What does it feel like to release?

The experience of releasing can widely vary depending on the individual. Most people feel an immediate sense of lightness or relaxation as they use the process. Others feel energy moving in their bodies as though they are coming back to life. You will also notice that your mind gets progressively quieter and your remaining thoughts clearer. You will start to see more solutions rather than just problems. Over time it may even feel positively blissful. The changes become more pronounced the longer you practice.

## How do I know I'm doing it right?

If you notice any positive shifts in feeling, attitude, or behavior, then you are doing it right. However, every issue you work on may require different amounts of releasing. If at first it doesn't shift completely, release and release again. Continue releasing until you have achieved your desired result.

## What if I feel I don't know how to release?

We were all born with the innate ability to let go. If you have ever watched a happy baby you know what I mean. Because this ability was not under our conscious control, over time we forgot how to do it. However, it is so natural that it doesn't require thinking, just as we don't think, "breathe," every time we take a breath.

Another way to look at it is with the example of a light

switch. The first time you turned a light switch did you know how it worked? Probably not. Nevertheless, the light turned on and you were able to experience the benefit of the light right away, before you ever understood how it operated.

The more you can lead with your heart and not your mind in this process, the easier it is to do. If you find you are getting stuck in wanting to figure it out, try letting go of the wanting to figure it out, and see what happens.

## How could something this simple be so powerful?

The most powerful and usable things in life are often the simplest. When things are allowed to remain simple, they are easy to remember and duplicate.

No one has to convince you how critically important breathing is, yet if I were to give you a procedure to follow for breathing it would be: "Breathe in–breathe out. Repeat as needed." What could be simpler? Yet there is little that is more fundamental to your life. As you use Holistic Releasing™ over time, you will discover that it can become as easy as second nature and require as little thought as breathing does now.

## What should I do if I find myself getting caught up into old patterns of behavior or I just plain forget to release?

First, it is important to remember that this is to be expected and it's OK. Your ability to release will increase over time. When you recognize that there is a problem, you can always release now.

When learning to release, you may go through the following progression:

1. You will do things just the way you did them before and you

will only remember to release afterwards. The moment you recognize that there is a problem, simply release.

2. Over time, you will start to catch yourself in the middle, when you are involved in the old behavior pattern. You can release when you recognize that you are doing it again, and you will find that you are able to change the old pattern.

3. Over more time, you will catch yourself about to get caught up in the pattern again and you will release and not do it.

4. Finally, you won't even need to release about that particular tendency because you will have completely let it go.

If you allow yourself to be persistent, your attitude and effectiveness will eventually change for the better, even about long-standing problems. It is also helpful to schedule short releasing breaks throughout your day to remind yourself to release.

## Relax, Have Fun, and Enjoy

As you work through the book, you may find your life getting lighter and freer and more alive. You may also find that you start to uncover some of the universal truths for which you have been striving. Congratulations on beginning this journey to the place that you have never left–the heart of awareness. It is my sincerest hope that this material will quickly help you to discover and live a life filled with a happiness without sorrow, a joy without bounds, and a peace and bliss that surpass all understanding.

"The all-quiet state is such a tremendous state,

that it can never be put into words. The words

ecstasy, euphoria, bliss, nirvana don't describe

it really—they only allude to it."

Lester Levenson

# Session 1

# The Quiet Meditative State of Beingness

Man may be divided into three general categories of havingness, doingness, and Beingness. The lowest of the three is the havingness state. Man thinks that if only he could have, he would be happy. "If only I could have a million dollars, I would be the happiest person in the world! If only I could have a strong, healthy body. "If only I could have…"

The next higher state is a doingness state. Instead of saying, "If only I could have," we rise to the place where we want to go out and do, and we are capable of doing things in the world. There, we are more interested in doingness than we are in havingness.

The highest state is the Beingness realm. This is the state that I'm trying to get you into. Beingness will have no meaning until you experience it. Only then will you know what it is, and you will want Beingness more than anything else in the world. This reminds me of something one of you said to me: "We visited a friend we hadn't seen for over a year. She's very interested in metaphysics. While we were visiting her, she said, 'Let's cut out this talking; let's meditate.

Why waste time talking?'"

She had already experienced this realm of Beingness. When you're up there, it looks silly to talk. Why talk? Why not just be?

Havingness is the category that roughly 90% of us are mostly in. "Oh, if we only could have those almighty dollars, more and more of them, or a million of them, then we would be free and happy." But what is the experience of those who do accumulate a million or more? Are they happy? No, they have many, many problems and are loaded down with non-freedom, more unhappy than happy.

The proof of their not attaining happiness is their compulsive drive to get more and more, even though they cannot use up the amount already accumulated. Were it true that material things brought happiness, the wealthy would be so over-happy that they would be incapacitated by it, and the poor would be so miserable that life would not be worth living.

The next higher state is the doingness state. Here we are the real doers in the world, and here are the leaders. Here we are found as big businessmen, small businessmen, big politicians and small politicians, people in the arts, and professional men. ("Men" includes men and women.) Here we are out on our own, more independent than the job holder. Are we happy? No? Happier than the job holder, because we're more independent, but still not free. We are yet compulsively driven.

I think the proof of this is the number of actors and actresses who, on attaining the height of fame and fortune, find themselves so unhappy that they commit suicide or go through life frustrated. We come now to the only state that can give us happiness with no sorrow–the state of Beingness. Beingness is the highest of the three states, and it is the very highest state possible. In the ultimate state, we are Beingness, being all Beingness. Stated another way, it's Awareness, aware of all Awareness. When we are just that, when we are only that, that's the highest state. It is in this top state of Beingness that we reach our ultimate of perfect contentment, perfect satiation, perfect joy, perfect peace. It is the state of highest felicity.

There's no giving up of anything on this path. You always take on more. Those who tell me, "Well, I don't want to give up" are refusing to hear what I have been saying. But why don't you hear it? It is very subtle ego-sabotage, saying, "I don't want to grow any more."

When this happens, I should present it to you so that you may see the ego-sabotage. Then you may let go of it and go further. We're moving toward an infinity, and until we are absolute and infinite, we should keep moving—if we want the ultimate happiness, and who doesn't?

We will never be fully happy until we reach that state. The ultimate happiness and your Self turn out to be one and the same thing. There will always be a subconscious, below the surface, a nagging that pushes us on until we achieve it, until we are there. What the world today calls happiness is escape from misery, alleviation of misery. The relatively small amount of happiness the world has is only relief from misery. All entertainment, all socializing is relief and escape from our thoughts! Look at, examine, and discover this. Stop chasing rainbows!

In the havingness state, one has the least happiness; in the doingness state, one has more happiness; in the Beingness state, one has the greatest happiness. I can't tell you what it is; it's an experience, and you just must experience it. The best way I can help you to experience it is to get you to do that which will put you into that state. It is a very deep, quiet, meditative state; it's a state wherein we let go of thoughts. Through my helping to guide you in such a way that you may fall into it, you can experience and know what this state of Beingness is. That guidance is to lead you into right meditation and to support you while in it.

My object is to try to show you how to get a deeper and deeper feeling of this state of Beingness. Now, some of us have gone very deep into the state of Beingness and know what it is. Yet, if I asked you to describe it, you'd have difficulty; you couldn't tell what it is. You could talk around it, describe it by saying it's nice, it's peaceful, serene, delightful. But what is it? You can't put it into words. It's like trying to explain to someone what an orange tastes like; you just cannot do it. Once one tastes the orange, then one knows. It's the same with this deep meditative state of Beingness. Once you taste it, you know it. And after you have tasted the deep state of meditative Beingness, you will want it more than anything else in the world.

You should meditate at least one hour in the morning and one hour before retiring. The morning meditation sets you in a mood and prepares you for a better day. The evening meditation helps undo the turbulence of the day and carries you through the night. You'll find yourself sleeping better. Increase the length of your set time of meditation until the meditative state stays with you all the time, until it remains with no effort. When you want this more than anything else in the world, you've gone deeply into your Beingness, into your Self.

This experience is so far greater than anything else you've ever experienced, you'll just prefer it to anything and everything else. Then you'll see and know that this is what you've been blindly seeking for in the world–looking for it through indirect means, through external means–and now that you've discovered that it's right where you are, you don't have to have anything, you don't have to do anything. You only have to just be what you are. It's your natural state!

I have not spoken about ways and means of meditation. I haven't been asked questions on it except, "What is meditation?"

Q: Do you want questions on it? Is that what you want?

Lester: That is up to you. I know that some of you joined Self Realization Fellowship and are beginning to get some of the methods. SRF's root teaching is meditation: how to meditate and how to do those things that will prepare you for meditation. It has many methods and means of helping one meditate better.

When thoughts come into our mind unwanted, when we cannot keep them out, we are far from being free. When we, at will, can cause thoughts to enter or not enter, then we are free and a master over mind. Until then, the mind is the master, and we are the slave; we are victims of our thoughts. We are actually being pushed around like automatons by our habit-thoughts.

People talk to us, and it's just as though they are pressing our automatic buttons. They praise us and we go up; they berate us, and we go down–like an automatic robot–and we think we're free-willed! Anyone who goes up on praise and down on condemnation is behaving like a robot, because whether I praise you or condemn you, I don't do a thing to you but send out tiny bits of sound, energy, and you give it enough power to make you happy or miserable, making you nothing but an automatic robot.

Now, an easy way to become master over your mind is through meditation. It's the practice of quieting the mind by seeking that which we really are. This we should do until we reach the goal. Our direction from here on should be learning how to meditate better. I can give far more potent guidance while you're in the meditative state than I could through my voice, but you will never know it until you experience it. The help you've gotten so far is small in comparison to the help you can receive when you get quiet. Then I can communicate to you directly, Self to Self. Then I can help you be your real Self–and not only I but also the Masters. Whether they're here in body or not, this is exactly what they do.

When we are quiet, They come in, and they help establish us in our Self. And by our experiencing it, we go deeper and deeper until it's complete, until we're in the quiet, meditative state twenty-four hours a day, regardless of what we are doing. In this quiet state, you never lose consciousness. When you go to sleep, you're fully aware that you're sleeping. When you are dreaming, you're fully aware that you're dreaming. Should you decide to cut the dream, you can cut the dream. The same with the sleep. Or, while you're fully awake, if you decide to go to sleep this moment, you go to sleep this moment.

This is not giving up anything. This is becoming a master over the three usual states that we all go through every day: the waking state, the dream state, and the deep, dreamless sleep state. I am summing up what has happened since I started with you. First, we worked to increase our havingness, then our doingness, and now we're with the top state of Beingness. The Beingness state should be developed from here on. Any questions about what I've been saying to you? Is it understood?

Q: The main purpose of meditation is to learn to quiet the mind?

Lester: Right. Purely, simply, and wholly to quiet the mind until it's totally quiet. When it's totally quiet, that's the goal. Every thought is a thing of limitation, is a cover, a veil, over our infinite Beingness. When we remove all the veils, there's nothing left but our infinite Beingness. The veils are only our thoughts. Mind is not mysterious—except when you don't understand it. When you understand, it's nothing but thoughts; it's as simple as that. It's the sum total collection of thoughts that is called mind. Stop the thoughts, and there's no more mind action. Meditation is simply a method of quieting the thoughts, and meditation should be continued until all thoughts are quieted.

The all-quiet state is such a tremendous state that it can never be put into words. The words ecstasy, euphoria, bliss, nirvana, don't describe it really; they allude to it. But, as I said, when you once experience a certain depth of meditation, you have experienced the greatest thing you ever have experienced in your life. And you will want to repeat that experience, want to establish and maintain it so that it is all the time. This experiencing turns out to be only your very own real Self, now called happiness—and indulged in very minutely.

When you gain this beautiful depth of quietude, don't spill it out in conversation. You don't see how much you let go of this beautiful quietude when you pour it out, lose it, in conversation. You get involved in thoughts, and the thoughts take you away from it. Then you have only the memory that it was a nice feeling. That feeling should be maintained, sustained, and retained. The best way to do this, after group meditation, is to go right home with it.

If you obtain it by yourself, remain by yourself. Just keep quiet; stay in it as long as you possibly can, until you become fully established in it all the time. Then it's all right to talk; you won't lose it.

But as it is now, you let go of the depth of quietude you get in meditation when you talk to people. You just waste it. It's so valuable to get that feeling. Hold it and develop it further and further, until it is there all the time. You'll know when the state of Beingness is complete when you see yourself as all Beingness.

First, we get a little of this beautiful state of quietness, peace, serenity, tranquility; then, as it develops, we begin to see more and more that we are all Beingness. In the beginning, it might be a flash, or for a minute, or five minutes; each time the concept will stay longer and longer until it's the only thing. Then you see yourself only as Beingness being all Beingness. Then you'll know what God is; you will know your real Self.

Q: This whole thing is like trying to tell somebody what the orange tastes like?

Lester: Yes, but most of us have experienced this quietude of Beingness to a degree, so it has a certain amount of meaning. To the degree that each one has experienced it, it has that much meaning to him. Then I add to it by saying: someday, you're going to have such a tremendous experience of just Beingness that, after it, you will want only to re-establish it permanently. Everything else in the world becomes secondary to it. You also recognize that what you have been seeking in the world is right where you are. It's not out there—it's within, right where you are. It's your natural, inherent state. It's your Self, and it's all the glory of gloriousness.

Q: Can this state be reached without direct conscious effort toward finding out who you are?

Lester: Yes, in a slower way, by seeking God through devotion and self-surrender. Surrender yourself wholly and completely unto your God, and you will reach it.

Q: I am trying to understand where I am now.

Lester: Okay, I'll tell you where you are now. You are at that place that's equal to how well you can remain quiet. To the degree that you can remain quiet, imperturbable—to that degree is your growth. In meditation, how well you can keep your mind on one thought without other thoughts coming in shows you how far you've gone. Your mind is much quieter now than it was when I met you. Are you aware of that?

Q: Well, I'm experiencing thought, so I can't see it.

Lester: There are indirect ways of telling: how easily you're disturbed by others, how much you react to what people say, and so forth. When your mind is really quiet, it doesn't matter what people say about you; you don't mind.

Q: But you already are that which you are seeking. It's just a matter of knowing it, isn't it?

Lester: Yes, it's a matter of re-remembering it, recognizing it. We have to experience it to recognize it. Meditation is the way to experience it. Right now, we're convinced that we're limited to being our body. That's the biggest lie of all lies; we're infinite! It's just a wrong perception, a wrong seeing. It's an illusion, it isn't real. The reality is that we are the Beingness behind the body.

Q: What we really should do when we get into meditation is to see what we are and not see the limited being, to get away from the sense of limitation?

Lester: Yes, let go of the concepts of limitation. By so doing, you experience Beingness more and more until you experience only the Being, You, just behind the body and mind.

Q: Our thoughts of limitation are what's restricting us from seeing what we are?

Lester: Yes, our thoughts, which themselves are limitations. Not our thoughts of limitation, but our thoughts—every one of which is a limitation.

Q: How do you differentiate between consciousness and thought?

Lester: Consciousness is general awareness. Thought is awareness of a particular thing.

Q: To me it means more if, instead of using the word "meditation," you would say, "I want you to begin getting rid of your sense of limitation and get a feeling of being All—that you are all knowledge, all consciousness."

Lester: That is what meditation does and achieves.

Q: I have to put it into words, and I suppose you know it instinctively.

Lester: No, I put it into words. I define meditation as keeping your mind on one thought. Now this makes sense to you: hold one thought such as, "What is God?" Just stay with that thought and only that thought, and keep other thoughts out: that's meditation. Take another thought, "What is this world?" and just hold that thought, "What is this world? By golly, what is it?"

You keep questioning, "What is this world?" When there is only one thought, the mind is quiet. When the mind is quiet, the answer comes from beyond the mind.

Q: You are not saying what we have been taught elsewhere, to think about a rose and not let any other thought come in. You're really saying, "Think about God," or about "It."

Lester: Yes. The very top question is, "What am I?" When the answer to that comes fully, that's it. By holding that question in your mind and awaiting the answer to it, you are doing the very best of meditation. No matter what method one uses, no matter what path he takes, in the end he gets the answer to "What am I?"

But know this: the mind will never give you the answer. Any answer the mind gives has to be wrong, because the mind is an instrument of thought, and every thought is limited. Therefore, you mentally pose the question, and you await the answer, and it is from beyond your mind, from your Self, that it comes.

Q: Because you already know, so you just stop the nonsense?

Lester: Yes, you stop the nonsense of not knowing.

Q: And, in recognizing, "I know, I know," I'm getting rid of being limited.

Lester: That's it! That's the whole thing in a nutshell. As you said, you already know it, and you just let go of the thoughts contrary to it until this knowingness is self-obvious. This is called realization or revelation.

Q: Is Beingness no thought of consciousness?

Lester: Beingness, when complete, is without thought. However, Beingness and consciousness are the same, which one cannot intellectualize on, but which one can experience. Beingness and consciousness are the exact same thing. That's why I said if you want to know a cow, be a cow. If you want to know what a tree is, be a tree. And you can, because you are. How better can you know something than to be it? The real answer will come when you get there; then you'll see that Beingness and consciousness are the same. Don't intellectualize on it; do it. Be it.

Q: It's awfully blah when, in meditation, nothing comes.

Lester: It shouldn't be blah, because, as you're doing it, you're quieting thoughts. The more you quiet thoughts, the happier you are.

I think by now we can all examine and know what our joys really consist of. If we're listening to music, our mind gets concentrated only on the music. All the other thoughts and problems of the day are let go of, and so the music seems beautiful. If we're thinking of the one we love, the same thing happens: our mind is only on that person, and all the other thoughts and troubles drop away, so loving that person is beautiful. It is really the dropping of our discomforting thoughts that makes the focus of our attention on something external seem so wonderful.

Q: I must express a thought I just had when you were talking. In other words, it's like all the electricity going one way, with no side issues, no interference. When you listen to music, you think about nothing but the music.

Lester: Yes, all other thoughts–bothersome limitations–are let go of for the time being, and you feel your real Self much more. You'll never know the real beauty until you see the beauty behind the beauty, the source of the beauty.

Q: Which is "I"?

Lester: Yes, your real Self.

Q: I now know what you're talking about when you use the word "meditation."

Lester: When you develop it, it leads you into the most beatific, blessed state; into nirvana, tranquility, and serenity; into your quiet meditative state of knowing what you are–You, the real Being of the universe, being your infinite, glorious and magnificent Self.

## Comments:

Allow yourself to go deeper. Most of us stay on the surface of what we call the world, our life, and our experience, even during meditation. We don't look below the surface. Part of this has to do with the fact that we are afraid of what we will find. We have been lead to believe that if we go deeper into our awareness we will discover our dark side or our negativity. In my experience working with thousands of people with the Sedona Method, even our deepest, darkest negativity is just on the surface.

All of our problems and negativity have as much substance as a soap bubble. What happens if you poke your finger into a soap bubble? Right. It goes pop, revealing its lack of substance. You will find that the same thing happens if you are willing to go to your real essential core. You will discover what Lester and I have been talking about in this book: Beingness, your Self.

## Suggestions for the week:

Here is a way to go deeper into your practice of self-inquiry. Ask yourself the question: "What am I?" Whatever arises as an answer, whether it is in the form of a thought, feeling, or experience, ask yourself: "If it is deeper than that, what am I?" and, "If is deeper than that, what am I?" Keep going deeper until you feel that you can go no further. Then allow yourself to rest as the silence as long as you can.

You can also use this question as you move through life. If you are getting lost in a train of thought or in a feeling, ask yourself: "What is deeper than that?" and "What is even deeper than that?" Keep going with these questions until you are at rest as the silent Beingness that you have always been. This exercise will help you to start living more of the time as Beingness, rather than only when you are in what you call meditation.

You may also want to explore these polarities:

• What is on the surface? –What is at the core?

• Where do the surface end and the core begin? –Where do the core end and the surface begin?

• Could I allow there to be as much noise as there is? –Could I allow there to be as much silence as there is?

The next seven pages of this book are designed to help further your own exploration. You can view them as your diary of progress during the week that you are working with this session. Use the space allowed on each page to write down your gains and realizations as they happen, as well as for notes on working with the various exercises.

# Day One

# Day Two

# Day Three

# Day Four

# Day Five

# Day Six

# Day Seven

"A person can control a whole nation,

but if they cannot control their own mind,

what kind of control do they have?

They are victims of their own mind."

Lester Levenson

# Session 2

# Meditation

The greatest thing, and the most difficult thing we have to do is to drop the mind. It's a junkyard full of refuse from ages past, a refuse of thoughts of limitations: I am a limited body; I have troubles. All thoughts contain limitation. We pile them up in the thing we call mind. Mind is nothing but the total accumulation of all these thoughts. So, mind is nothing but a junkyard of limitation.

All right, so how do we get rid of the mind? By quieting it. When we quiet the mind, we discover our infinity. The more we see our limitlessness, the more we recognize that junkyard called mind–and the more we let go of it–until we go so far that we drop the whole remaining mind at one time. However, before that, we keep battling the thoughts as they come up. As the thoughts come up, we let go, let go, let go, until we let go of enough of them so that the Self that we are is obvious. Then it takes over and takes us all the way. The greatest thing is quieting the mind, which is eliminating thought, eliminating the mind.

Meditation is necessary. This is the major point I'm stressing: meditation. Learn how to meditate. The deeper one goes, the more one discovers the innate joys to which there are no limits. No matter how joyful you get, you can always go further. If you were a thousand times more joyful than you are now, you could still go on and on and on in joy. Joy is unlimited because we're infinite. But the major thing to accomplish is the ability to control the mind, to meditate, to drop into peace at will.

A man can control a whole nation, and if he cannot control his own mind, what kind of control has he got? He is a victim of his own mind. Rather than being in free control over his thoughts, he is an effect of them. He is actually pushed around by past habits. He is no Master. Only he who can control his mind is a Master, a Master not only of himself, but of anything and everything he does. Meditation is the way.

The remainder of this session is composed of aphorisms collected from various talks by Lester. Allow yourself to spend as much time as you need pondering each statement before you move on to the next.

- Meditation is directed thinking.

- Meditation is putting your mind on the way to find God.

- Meditation is looking for the answers in the right direction.

- Meditation is basically thinking in the right direction and holding to it so that other thoughts keep dropping away until the mind is concentrated. When the mind is concentrated, the answers become obvious to you.

- Concentration is holding one thought to the exclusion of other thoughts that will lift one and help one grow.

- The ability to hold one thought concentrates the mind so that it can crack the secrets of itself.

- Meditating to get the mind quiet is good. Meditating to let go of ego-wants is better. Meditating on "What am I?" is best.

- Meditate, actively seeking.

- Meditation should be on: "What am I? What is God? What is the world? What's my relationship to the world? What is the substance of this world? What is infinity? What is intelligence? Where is this world?" Or you can also meditate on some of the statements you've heard, like, "I'm not in the world, but the world is in me." Then ask, "How come?" Try to see it. Try to see the meaning behind these statements of truth.

- We get to see the perfection by looking in the direction where the perfection is. Now, the perfection isn't out there; we know that. The perfection is in here where we are, where the "I" of us is. So, first we have to direct our attention inwardly. We should pose a question and hold it until the answer comes. When the answer does come, you know, and you know you know. To get the answer to, "What am I?" it is necessary to still the noise of the mind, to still the thoughts. The thoughts are the noise. The thoughts are concepts of limitation, and there are so many of them that they're constantly bombarding us, one after another all the time. Keep on dropping them until the perfection is obvious.

- All these extraneous thoughts wouldn't come in if we weren't interested in them.

- We must learn how to quiet the mind. We can never learn how by constant conversation. The less conversation, the better.

- Meditation does not have to be formal to be meditation. It can be any time one gets quiet and seeks. Some of us find it is easier to meditate when it isn't formal, because sometimes we unconsciously have objections and resistances to formal meditation. However, we should work to drop the objections and resistances and be free of them.

- Reverse your negative thoughts as they come into mind. Let go of negative thoughts by reversing them, and then, eventually, let go of all thoughts.

- What you gain remains. Even though you've undone one thought, one idea, there still remains multitudes of thoughts, and so another one comes up. Undoing one limiting thought doesn't undo all the subconscious thoughts. What remains must be let go of. By dropping a tendency or predisposition, you drop all the thoughts motivating it.

- Everything that everyone is looking for through work is far better gotten through meditation. Meditation will sooner and

better get you what you want than working in the world, for
it will.

- It is the doorway to the Infinite when you go inward. When
you go outward, it is the doorway to limitation.

- Internalize your attention. All externalized attention is wasted.

- What you do to yourself, being your own doing, can only be
undone by you.

- God is known only through your effort and direction. Look
concentratedly within for the kingdom of God.

- With meditation, you will discover that you've covered up
your unlimited Self with your limited ego.

- Meditation is the road to omnipresence.

- Meditate to get into the practice and habit of meditation. We
should meditate as much as we possibly can. Meditation is
getting the mind one-pointed in the direction of who and
what we are. It's taking the mind away from the worldly things
and focusing it on the direction that we're in. The more we
do it, the more we like it. And the more we like it, the more
we do it, until it becomes a thing that goes on effortlessly all
the time. No matter what you're doing, that meditation continues in the background. Then you are really moving. Until
then, you're not moving very rapidly, because most of the

time you're in the world and in the direction of limitation.

There's only one way to get to the high state and that is by quieting the mind. The method of quieting the mind is meditation. It's very difficult: the moment you sit down and want to quiet the mind, up pop the thoughts. Well, as the thoughts pop up, keep knocking them out, putting them out, dropping them, until you reach a state where you can sit relatively quiet. Then you begin to like meditation, because it's a deeper experience of your real Self.

Once you like it, the main obstacle to the practice of meditation is eliminated. But you should never stop until you reach the place where meditation is delightful. Then you will go on with ease.

- The most effective meditation is when you are by yourself. Group meditation is for beginners, for the purpose of accustoming one to meditation.

- Meditation really should be communing with your Self.

- You'll see your Self to the proportion that your mind is quiet.

- The way to get rid of the ego is to get the mind so quiet that you can see what you are. Then you know that you are not the ego, and you drop it.

- Intense meditation will get you to your realized teacher, to your Master.

- To expand out from being just a body is so difficult because of the state of the world today. We do need the help of the Masters to lift us, actually to help pull us right out of it. They cannot do that unless we are receptive. We cannot be receptive unless our mind is quiet, and our mind becomes quiet through meditation.

- Just go into meditation–get quiet and expect that higher help, and it will come. God and Gurus are constantly helping us. If we just get quiet, with their help, we are lifted into experiencing our Self.

- Meditation has to get to the point where it is the most important thing. However, even a little meditation will go a long way, especially if it is concentrated.

- Spiritual things are spiritually discerned. Spiritual knowledge does not come down to a lower level. We have to raise ourselves up to it. We raise ourselves in meditation. Meditation should be used to get higher understanding by raising ourselves up to where higher understanding is.

- Meditation is wonderful. Things happen in meditation that never could happen while you are talking or active.

- You can make the mind quiet by the desire to discover what you are. When the interest in knowing what you are becomes stronger than the interest in this world and body, then you discover You. Desire–intense desire for it–is the key.

- The concept of meditating by making your mind a blank is in error. You cannot make your mind a blank.

- Meditation is a stepping stone to the knowledge of the answer to, "What am I?"

- Someday, the most delightful thing you will know of will be meditation.

- Meditate until it becomes constant, i.e., until it continues in back of the mind regardless of what you are doing.

- There is a meditation of just getting quiet. Just get quiet, not in a passive way, but in an active way of just being. It's awfully nice to just be and be and be. It's a tremendous experience. It's a wonderful feeling of just being. However, don't stop there. Keep dropping ego until there is no more.

- You'll reach a point where you'll like meditation better than anything else, because you'll reach a point where you're being very much your real Self.

    That is the greatest of all joy which you formerly thought was external in the world, in your wife, in your children. You'll see your wife and your children as nothing but your very own Self; you'll see that. And the joy will be direct and constant all the time.

- The answer won't come from reasoning. It will come from quiet meditation. Some day, some time, it will come. It will just present itself to you, so simple, and you'll say, "Oh!"

• Meditation is thinking, but thinking on one thing so that other thoughts drop away. When you are intensely interested in one thing, other thoughts drop away.

• The quieter we are, the more we are the Self. When meditation becomes constant, all the time, even though we are outwardly active, we go through life and work automatically, all the time remaining in our real Self.

• The mature seeker of the Self starts with, "The reality is that I was never bound. I was always free and perfect," and takes off from there.

• Just look at what you are instead of what you are not. When you discover what you are, you simultaneously discover what you are not and drop it.

• Say, "I am not this body; I am not this mind," and stay with it.

• Seeing that you're not the ego, you're letting go of big chunks of ego.

• The depth to which you go in meditation determines how much you wipe out the ego.

• Depth of meditation is the degree of quieting the mind.

- The longer you can meditate, the deeper you can go.

- Once you reach peace, then find out what you are.

- Getting the good feeling is good. The higher you go, the better the feeling is. But when you look for the good feeling as the end, then that is the end. Growing is more than dropping into the good feeling of the Self; it is dropping the non-self, the ego.

- Enjoying meditation is a step, but don't stop there—go beyond it. You have got to get the answer.

- One could possibly meditate forever and forever.

- Meditation in itself can get to be a trap, can be used as a crutch. You've got to get realizations.

- When you get full realization, you're in the meditative state all the time. Actually, meditation is the natural state.

- Constant meditation is a constant remembering of God, of Self.

- Meditation is extremely difficult at first, but it gets easier as time goes on. Then one day you'll say, "This is great! This is what I want!" Then you do it all the time. Then you're really on the spiritual path.

- With complete concentration, dwell upon your Self. Turn the mind back upon the mind to discover what the mind is, and then go beyond the mind and dwell in your Self. Each one must experience it. It's a perception, but it's not really a mental perception. You get recognitions, revelations, and realizations by keeping the mind pointed in one direction until it gets very quiet, until other thoughts drop away. Hold one thought until it takes you to the realm just behind thinkingness. The answer is there. We call it an experience, a revelation.

- We must learn to quiet the mind so that when we sit down, we let go of the world. Only then do we really begin to move at high levels on this spiritual path. We've made this world a better world; we've made this dream a happier dream, but we're almost as bound as we were before. We have replaced bondage to bad things with bondage to good things. Now we must learn to let go of thoughts, all thoughts. The way is through meditation, right meditation: quieting the mind, stilling the thoughts, and, finally, eliminating all thoughts.

- In group meditation, support is lent one unto the other. The power is multiplied, and you can get more deeply quiet as time goes by. But the very best meditation is when you are by yourself, and you need no group support. Then you are not confined to any time period. You get with it, and you might stay with it five, ten, even twenty-four hours. And this should happen. When you get to like it so much that you stay up all night continuing it, it has become more interesting than sleep. Then you've got the momentum going. Then you'll get to see and be your real Self.

- A way to dominate the mind is to drop into the Self. You reach a place where it's so delightful you just don't want to do anything but remain in it. It gets to be very easy. Once you get to the point where it's easy, then just continue it. Stay with it until you go all the way. By the constancy of it, each day, you get quieter and quieter, and then the Self, as you see it, keeps scorching the ego, which further quiets the mind.

- You know, it's said that your spiritual growth really begins when you are able to drop into samadhi. I don't like to say this, because it's discouraging to some people. Samadhi is complete absorption in your thought. It's total concentration.

- Meditation at first is holding the thoughts on God, Self, to the exclusion of other thoughts. When one is realized, meditation is the awareness—not of anything by anyone, but only the current of awareness where there is no otherness and no action, yet is compatible with the full use of the mental and physical faculties.

- At the end of the road of meditation, you discover your grand and glorious Self!

Comments:

When these sessions were written, Lester felt that meditation was the highest path to freedom. As he worked with people and meditation, however, he discovered that for most it was not enough. He had students that could easily meditate eight hours a day or more, who would plateau and not keep moving forward. That is why he started looking for a better way to quiet the mind. This was the inspiration for the creation of the Sedona Method. The Sedona Method is like meditation in action. So it can easily be maintained twenty-four hours a day. It is a form of self-inquiry that is uniquely suited to the western mind. If you are currently involved in any meditation practice that you feel is benefiting you, please use our material to support you in gaining even more from your meditations.

## Suggestions for the week:

The following exercise is not the Sedona Method, but it will give you a sense of what the Sedona Method is about and help you to get into the habit of dropping the mind all the time and resting as the Self.

As you sit in meditation and as you move through life, thoughts and feelings that you can get lost in, or that can dictate how you feel and act arise in your consciousness. When you catch yourself being disturbed or held back by your thoughts and feelings, you can simply let them go on the spot with this simple question: "Could I let this go?"

Now, I know this may seem too simple. Yet, if you allow yourself to do it with an open heart and mind and the determination to let go, you will find that you can easily drop even longstanding patterns of thought and feeling. As you discover you can let go, you will do it more and more, until letting go becomes as much as a habit as holding on is right now. Then you will find that you live much more of the time at rest as who and what you are.

You may also choose to explore the following polarities:

• I am bound–I have never been bound.

• I am the seeker–I am what is sought.

- There is an inside that is separate from outside–Inside and outside are just concepts; there is only one.

You may also want to explore this question: "If the reality is that I was never bound–I was always free and perfect–then what am I?"

The next seven pages of this book are designed to help further your own exploration. You can view them as your diary of progress during the week that you are working with this session. Use the space allowed on each page to write down your gains and realizations as they happen, as well as for notes on working with the various exercises.

# Day One

# Day Two

# Day Three

# Day Four

# Day Five

# Day Six

# Day Seven

"All of a sudden it's there and you realize it's
always been there, that you have been looking
away from it by deluding yourself into thinking
you are a body and mind."

Lester Levenson

# Session 3

# The Game

Since we have such a large and mixed group, I don't know how to start. The best thing is to do that which is best for the greatest number. There really is no mass teaching that is very effective. Teaching, in order to be really effective, must be on an individual basis. The power of the teacher when focused on a group is not nearly as powerful as when focused on an individual.

The power used by the Guru is more intense with the individual—it's dispersed to the group, it's not concentrated. When the Guru works with an individual pupil, all the power flows through to the pupil to lift him to the place where he sees the truth.

Now, each individual has a particular thing that he or she is seeking and needing at the moment. When I answer an individual on the point that he is asking, usually there are others who have the same question and who can benefit by it. Therefore, in general, I like to answer questions. But, if you want, I'll give you a short synopsis of the subject.

Basically, we are all infinite, perfect Beings. I assume that most of us accept this, at least theoretically. We are told this by the scriptures, especially the Hindu scriptures. The Masters tell us this. I come along and say the same thing. But why don't we express this infinite, perfect Being that we are?

The reason why we don't express it is that through the habit of lifetimes, we have played a game of limitation. We have played it so long that we have completely forgotten that we have been playing a game of limitation and that our real basic nature is infinite. We do not look at this infinite Being that we are. We continue, every day, every moment, looking at this little puppet that we set up called the body, and assume that we are that body. So long as we keep looking at this body as being us, we are stuck right there. We cannot see our infinity, we don't know that it is, and we go on and on, lifetime in and lifetime out, assuming that we are a body.

We have done this for so long that it takes a super will to move in the opposite direction, to look at and see the infinite Being that we really are. This super will can take us away from assuming every moment that we are a limited body. If we would do it for just one second and see this infinite Being that we really are, we would use that second to undo much limitation. But first we must assume that we are infinite. Then we must start undoing the limitations.

We must actually accept that we are not this body, that we are not this mind, and, until we do that, we have absolutely no chance of getting out of this trap called "The Game of Being Limited Bodies."

So, as the scriptures say, "Thou art that." Be still and know it. Every thought we have is necessarily a thought of limitation. Let go of thought–get still. The methods are, as we know, to get quiet. Quiet the mind. The moment the mind is quiet enough, this infinite Being that we are becomes self-obvious. So, the method is very simple: quiet that mind enough so that you see this infinite Being that you are.

Now, the moment you see it, the moment you see this infinite Being that you are, you'll immediately go to work to undo the remaining thoughts that you are not it. And when there are no more thoughts, there's only the infinite Being left. Very oddly, what you are seeking is the very closest thing to you. Every time you say "I," that's it. When you say "I," you're talking about the infinite Being. When you say, "I am a body," you're saying, "I, the infinite Being, am a limited body with a limited mind." It's really as simple as all that. But simplicity does not mean it's easy to let go of the habits that you have been hanging onto for eons.

This that everyone is seeking, the thing that everyone calls happiness, is nothing but the infinite Self that we are. Everyone, in his every act, is seeking this infinite Self that he is, calling it by other names: money, happiness, success, love, etc. Having been told this—and, again, we've been told this many times before—why don't we just be what we are and stop trying to be what we are not, a limited body? Can anyone answer that? Why don't we stop being limited?

Q: Because we can't.

Lester: You mean an infinite Being can't stop being limited?

Q: Because we don't want to.

Lester: Right. We don't want to!

Q: The infinite Being doesn't want to?

Lester: Yes. I, the infinite Being, think I am a limited body, and I've been doing this so long that I, the infinite Being, don't want to let go of constantly assuming I am this limited body. Does that make sense?

Q: Yes.

Lester: Every time you say "I" without going any further, you're talking about the infinite Being that you are, but you immediately add to it, "am this body." If you would only just say, "I, I, I," from hereon, you'd get full realization, because, as you're saying, "I, I, I," you're concentrating on "I" and not saying "am a little body with needs."

So, there's no one who is not every moment experiencing the infinite Being that he is. As long as he experiences an "I," he is experiencing this infinite Being that he is. However, you don't want to see that. You want to be the body.

So, what is required? First, saying to yourself, "I am not this body, I am not this mind; then what am I?" If we reject this body and mind enough, what we are becomes self-obvious. We can never become an infinite Being, because we are that. We can just let go of the concepts that we are not it. We can just let go of the concepts that we are a body, a mind.

The first thing needed is the desire to let go of this limited beingness that we think we are. A very strong desire to be the infinite Being that we really are is the only thing that we need to get there quickly. But we don't want it. If we really wanted it, we would have it. There is a difficulty, of course. And what is the difficulty? It's the habit; it's the unconscious habitual thinking. It's the mind. So we attack it by attacking this unconsciously always-thinking mind.

The mind is the only cover over the infinite Being that we are. We must stop thinking long enough to see what we are, and that "long enough" can be just one second. If you would stop thinking for one second (thinking includes the unconscious thinking, too), if you would stop thinking for one second, the tremendous liberating shock of seeing what you are would cause you to use this infinite power that is yours to scorch the mind. The mind can be scorched in large amounts, each and every time we will—just for a moment—drop into that unlimited state of no thinking.

I guess the next question is how do we create the desire for it? If the desire is strong enough, anyone can see and fully be the infinite Being in a matter of weeks, months, a few years. If anyone of you had a strong desire to see this infinite Being that you are and just kept that desire only, in a few months you would see and remain as the infinite Being that you are. You would stop imagining yourself to be a limited body.

The key is desire. When you desire to be a body beautiful, a body healthy, all these thoughts prevent you from seeing the infinite Being that you are. You simply must exchange all your desires for the one desire to discover your infinite, real Self. I'd like some questions now on what I've said, so I can get closer to your wishes.

Q: While doing "What am I?" I looked at the stars, and I got an idea that I could be the stars. Then I talked to someone else, and they said, "No, you don't do that." And I thought, "Well, for God's sakes, I am going to find out how to do it!"

Lester: We are talking about a method called Self-inquiry, which is really the very top method. The final question we all have to answer is: What am I? And when that answer comes, that's it. So why not pose that question at the beginning?

When you pose the question, "What am I?" whatever answer the mind gives cannot be right, because the mind is the cover over your real Self. The mind is the thing that limits you. The method is to hold only the question "What am I?" If another thought comes in, quickly stop it by saying to yourself, "To whom is this thought? Well, to me. Well, what am I?" And you're right back on the track.

Q: I see. Thank you.

Lester: Now, there are just a rare few on our planet that can successfully use that method. Therefore, I suggest we use it this way: always seek the answer to "What am I?" No matter what you do during the day–whether in meditation, reading, and so forth–in the back of your mind, always keep that question poised and posed, ready and waiting for an answer. "What am I? What am I?"

I use "what" rather than "who," because "who" is a personal pronoun that tends to lead us into being the body. "What" is more impersonal, but this question should always be held. No matter what path we follow, no matter what method we use, we should always hold in the background, "What am I?" And if we do that, eventually we must see the full answer. Did I answer your question?

Q: Yes you did, thank you.

Q: Lester, pertaining to that, how many times does one ask the question?

Lester: Every time a thought, a stray thought, comes into the mind, we must say, "To whom is this thought? Well, it's to me. Then, what am I?" This will have to be repeated after each stray thought.

Q: But if no thoughts come, then it's not to be said?

Lester: Right.

Q: You wait then for an answer.

Lester: Wait to see. You don't wait for an answer, an answer would come from the mind.

Q: You wait to see?

Lester: Yes, you wait to see. The Self becomes self-obvious. All of a sudden it's there, and you realize it has always been there, that you have been looking away from it by deluding yourself into thinking you're a body, a mind. And then you see yourself as all Beingness. You become every person, every animal, every insect, every atom in the universe.

That the Beingness of the universe is only your Beingness is what you discover. It's there; it's there right now! But you are looking away from it all the time. When the mind is quieted enough, it's there. It's the "I" that I am—that's it. There's nothing closer to you than that. Most of the time you are seeking it out there, through a body, and it isn't out there. It's the "I" in here that is the infinite Being.

Holding only that question is not easy, and therefore I suggest holding it in general. Get in the habit of always seeking what you are, no matter what method you're using. And when quietness of mind comes—to the degree that there's no other thought on your mind but "What am I?" —this stilling of all the other thoughts makes your Self self-obvious. It's right there where you are, wherever you are, right where the "I" is. So, again, hold that question—no matter what method you use—until the answer shows itself, until it becomes obvious.

Q: It seems very hard.

Lester: It's hard to let go of the habit of thinking every moment that you are a limited body. We're just bombarding ourselves all the time with the thought: I am a body, I am a body, I am a body. This goes on all the time, so that we don't see the infinite Being that we are. It's a constant bombardment of: I am a body with involvement. Meditation is an attempt to quiet the mind by holding one thought so that other thoughts die away. By holding that one thought—if we can get to the place where just that one thought is there—that's enough quieting to see the infinite Being that we are. There isn't a method that doesn't try to effect the quieting of the mind so that the infinite Being that we are can become self-obvious.

Q: When you say "self-obvious," what does your real Self feel like?

Lester: When you get toward the end, as Vivekananda said, you see that there never was anything but "I" all alone. Now, if there's nothing but "I" all alone, then "I am everything, everyone" is your feeling.

You look upon every other body as equally your body. You see everyone as you; just as you see your body as you, you see everyone as you. The feeling is indescribable. It's such an intense experience, far beyond anything that limitation today will allow, that you'll never know it without experiencing it. But, from the level where we are, it's the thing we call happiness. It's joy unlimited, infinite joy. At first it comes on as an elation: it's overwhelming; it's hard to contain. It gets to be uncomfortable. You get slap-happy, punch-drunk, ecstatic; it gets to be annoying.

And then you work at it until it falls away, and what's left is a very deep, profound, delectable peace. It's a peace that is so much better than the extreme joy that you had before that you don't look for that joy any more. The joy state is not the ultimate; the ultimate is the peace state. Everyone of us can get a taste of it at times.

Q: Then it's possible to come across this and then lose it?

Lester: Oh, yes. Many people do. The first time we really drop into it, we are not able to maintain it, because the habit of thinking takes over again. And the moment we're thinking, we are thinking we are limited. Every thought must be a thing of limitation. Let go of the game of being limited; let go of the world.

Don't try to control it. Don't try to enjoy it. Take all your joy from within. Then, what was formerly the game assumes a sameness picture. Everything becomes the same. If everything is the same, and it is in the absolute truth, where can there be a game? If you get caught up in a game, you're caught up in an eternal illusion. The game will never end. And if you're in the game, you're away from your infinite Beingness. There is always a certain limitation in the game that will always keep you from being fully satisfied.

So, there is a step above the game of playing we are bodies, and that step is where everything becomes exactly the same. And that exact sameness is only you, your Beingness. There's an infinite Oneness left, and that infinite Oneness is you and is your Beingness. It's Beingness being all Beingness.

And there's no separation; there's only Beingness, being all Beingness. Now, of course, it takes experiencing it to really know what this Beingness is. I am convinced that the best description of the top state is Beingness being all Beingness.

Q: How can I increase my desire for it?

Lester: Only you can do it. No one can do it for you. This is the unique thing about it. You have to do it. The grace we hear of is always existing. It's the inner Beingness that we are making us uncomfortable until we re-establish the original state. Desire for happiness is the grace. It's always there. All we need to do is to recognize it and take it.

Q: How does God get made into man? Isn't it somehow sacrilegious to try to change back?

Lester: No. Anyone who tells you that doesn't want you to attain the top state. But it happens this way: It's like going to sleep at night. You dream you're born into a little infant body; then you are a week old, a year old; then twenty, then forty. And you dream you have problems and problems and problems. Remember, this is only a night dream. This goes on and on, and you get so tired of it that you dream the body dies. Then you wake up.

Where did you ever change yourself while in that dream? You didn't! You say it never was; it was all concocted in my mind, right? That's exactly how we do it in this waking state. This waking state is a sleep state. We are totally asleep to the reality of this infinite Beingness that we are. We are no more awake to the truth right now than when we are asleep at night. We are just dreaming that we are awake.

Actually, this is a sleep state that we need to awaken from–and, when we do, then we say, "Oh, my gosh, it never was! I never was a limited body! I was always that infinite Being that I am!" So, we mentally create a dream called the waking state of the world. However, it's just a dream-illusion. But to recognize that it's a dream, you must wake up out of this state. Does that make sense? So, the answer to "How did we do this?" is that we are dreaming it!

Q: Deliberately?

Lester: Yes, deliberately. You see, we start off as infinite Beings in a passive way. We go down to the bottom–that's where we are now–then go back to the top and again see our infinity. But after going through that, there's a positive knowingness of our infinity, whereas before it was a passive knowingness. It's something like this: "Perfect health" is meaningless to someone who was born perfectly healthy and stays that way all his life. He doesn't positively know what it is. And yet, it's a nice state when he's in it. But he's passively healthy; he cannot fully appreciate it.

However, if he got very sick and was on the verge of dying for many years and then re-established the perfect-health state, then that perfect-health state would be far more meaningful to him than it was before he got sick. And this is the silly thing we do to ourselves: We go from infinity down to where we are and back up to infinity with a positiveness of knowing the infinity that we are. But we pushed, on the way down, in a way that we lost sight of what we were doing. And if we look within, we'll discover this.

Q: That's the first time I've heard a sensible explanation of the whole mess, the first time it's ever been explained why we've been pulled down.

Lester: Okay, now go back up.

Q: Is there one person doing this?

Lester: There is one Beingness doing this. I think the best example of this is that of the ocean and the drops. We, the ocean of Beingness, imagined little tiny circles around parts of us that we called drops; and this drop says, "I am separate from that drop and separate from all the other drops." It's an imagined circle around part of the ocean calling itself a drop, but, actually, every drop is the ocean. It has all the qualities of the ocean: it's wet, it's salty, it's $H_2O$, and so forth.

I think that example might make sense. Or, it's like a comb, and each tooth says to the other, "I am separate from you." It's all one comb, and we are the teeth saying that we are separate, when, in actuality, it's just one comb. Remember, you are the one infinite ocean of Beingness. It is the "I" that you are. Seek it, see it, and forever hold it!

Comments:

Would you rather play the game of limitation or would you rather be free? That simple question is a key to dropping our obsession with being limited body-minds. If you think you are your body-mind and the stories that you tell yourself and others about being that body-mind, then you would rather play the game of limitation. However, if you begin to recognize that you are not now and have never been that body-mind with all its limitations, then you have begun the process of waking up to your true nature. You would rather be free.

At first you may only want this freedom a little. But the more you taste it and live it, the more you will choose it over the game of limitation.

Suggestions for the week:

As you move through the game of life, whenever you find yourself taking it seriously or getting caught up in your story or your problems, ask yourself: "Would I rather play the game of life or would I rather be free?" When answered honestly with the response, "I would rather be free," this simple question will cause you spontaneously to drop your identification with the you that appears to be playing the game, as well as with your problems related to playing it.

If you find that you would rather play the game at that particular moment, then let yourself play it full tilt, doing your best to recognize it as a game. This will weaken your attachment and aversion to the story that we call the game of life.

You may also want to explore the following polarities:

• I am the limited body–I am infinite Beingness.

- I want to be the body–I want to just be.
- Everything is different–Everything is the same.
- The world is real–The world is just a dream that never really was.

You may also want to explore this question: "If there is only Beingness being all Beingness, then what am I?"

The next seven pages of this book are designed to help further your own exploration. You can view them as your diary of progress during the week that you are working with this session. Use the space allowed on each page to write down your gains and realizations as they happen, as well as for notes on working with the various exercises.

# Day One

# Day Two

# Day Three

# Day Four

# Day Five

# Day Six

# Day Seven

"The reason why so few of us make it is that most of us have a stronger subconscious desire to be a physical body than we have a conscious desire to be a free unlimited being."

Lester Levenson

# Session 4

# Realization by Dropping
# the Unconscious

Our subject is called many things by many schools. I like to call it happiness. That which gives you the ultimate in happiness is the discovery of the truth of you. Then you get to completely know you—you reach the ultimate joy, the peace of satiation. You discover that you are the All, and that your former worldly search was your trying to find your real Self in the world. There you never could discover the real you, the consequence of which was that you were never satisfied.

You are this thing called happiness. Your basic nature is infinite joy, far beyond anything your mind could comprehend. That's why everyone is seeking happiness. We're all trying to return to that wonderful inherent state that, when discovered, is ours all the time. However, we do not find it, because we are looking away from rather than toward it. We must look within. Basically, we are infinite Beings. We have no limitation, we have all knowledge; we have all power, and we are omnipresent, here and now.

There isn't anyone who doesn't possess these three things. The difficulty in discovering our purpose and goal in life is that, because we are infinite, we can make ourselves infinitely small. And this is exactly what we have done. We have achieved the extreme in limitation. We couldn't be much more limited than we are right now. In this universe, which is infinite in size, and in the three worlds, we are at the extremest end of limitation. We have imagined ourselves, and frozen ourselves, into physical bodies; and because of so many millennia of looking at ourselves as bodies, we have become convinced that we are these physical bodies.

Beings are capable of seeing all realms that are denser than theirs. In the subtlest realm–the causal world–Beings can perceive the denser astral and physical realms. In the astral world, Beings can perceive the denser physical world, and, because we are in the physical realm and cannot see a denser realm, we are in the densest, most limited realm possible. The physical body being the extremest end of limitation possible to us, we feel cramped: we hurt, we reach out. We try to express our freedom in the physical world. We try to eliminate time and space, to go faster and further.

I'm pointing out how far we have gone in accepting limitation since we came into a physical body, and that this is the reason why it is so difficult for most of us to discover the truth of ourselves, which is we have no limits. However, there's an advantage to being in this very limited state. Because we are so cramped, we have more of a desire to get out of it than we would if we were living in a harmonious heaven where everything was easy and immediately available–where life does not prod us into trying to get liberation.

We have a very distinct advantage in being here. We are forced to seek a way out. We are trying in many ways and with many methods to get free. No matter what the methods are, they all must end up doing the very same thing: freeing us of our concepts of limitation.

The methodology must quiet our mind, must do away with thoughts. Every thought is a concept of limitation. When thoughts are undone, what's left over is the infinite Being that we are.

Unfortunately, we set into motion an automatic way of thinking called the subconscious mind. There, we relegate thoughts to the background and let them operate without needing to pay any attention to them. And we have lost sight of them. In the beginning, it was an advantage in operating a physical body, because originally we had to operate every part of the body consciously—every cell, every organ and to eliminate all that attention, we put it on automatic control via the subconscious mind, and the subconscious mind is the real difficulty when we try to let go of thoughts.

It's difficult, because we are in the habit of not looking at it. Not looking at it, we don't see it. Since we don't see it, it goes on and on, lifetime in and lifetime out. We are so married to our thoughts that we never even think of divorcing them. And, until we do, we will continue, blindly attached to physical bodies and, in the overall, having a miserable life.

For every ounce of pleasure we take, we get pounds of pain; and it must be that way, because the pleasure we are trying to get is by seeking our very own Self externally in the world and through the body. And it just isn't there. The methods to be effective must be in a direction of first quieting our thoughts, then actually getting rid of our thoughts. Make a conscious effort to bring up subconscious thoughts and, when they are brought to the conscious plane, drop them. When they do come up, because they are very limiting and very negative as a whole, you want to drop them—and you do.

After you have dropped an appreciable number of them, then you can drop thoughts in larger amounts. To drop thoughts in larger amounts requires dropping the tendency or predisposition that has evolved from the accumulated thoughts on that one particular thing. Dropping the tendency or predisposition, one drops all the thoughts that caused that tendency or predisposition. In this way you may, at one time, drop a large accumulation of thoughts.

For instance, if one has a tendency to like sweets, one could bring up from the subconscious one thought at a time and continue letting go of them until there are no more. This takes a lot of time. However, if one drops the tendency itself, then all the subconscious thoughts that make up that tendency are dropped, and one is totally free from desiring sweets. Later, you reach a point where you can drop all the remaining thoughts at once, because having infinite power, you will have reached the point where you can see that you have this infinite power, and you then can use it to wipe out the rest of the mind. That is why it is sometimes said that realization is instantaneous.

When you get that far, that you can see that the power is yours, you wipe out all the remaining thoughts at once. Then you are totally free; you've gone all the way. When this happens, you don't become a zombie, and you don't disappear or go up in a flash of light. What you do is let the body go through that which you preset for it; and when you reach the end of the line of the action for the body, you will leave it with joy. You will leave it just the way you leave and let go of an old, worn out overcoat.

You will never die. People around you might say so, but to yourself, you don't die. You consciously drop the body the way you would drop an old, worn out overcoat. But, again, you won't do this until you run the course that you preset for it.

Now, I tell you this so you won't be fearful of dying if you get realization. So, attaining the ultimate state is not disappearing into a nothingness–it's a moving out into your omnipresence and letting go of confinement to only a physical body.

Now, to do this, you must have a strong desire to do it. The only thing that keeps you from being the infinite Being that you are is your desire to be a limited physical body. When your desire shifts into wanting to get free of the extreme limitation, it's a start; but to go all the way, you must have a desire to be totally free that is more intense than your desire to be a physical body. The reason why so few of us make it is that most of us have a stronger subconscious desire to be a physical body than we have a conscious desire to be a free, unlimited Being.

Until you confront this and see what your desire really is, it is impossible to achieve total freedom, total realization. You should dig into the subconscious to bring up your desires, because, unless you see them, you can't let go of them. The only reason why you are limited to the physical body is that, subconsciously, you have a strong desire to be this limited physical body. When your conscious desire to be free becomes stronger than your subconscious desire to be a physical body, then you'll quickly achieve your freedom. And therein lies your ultimate happiness. I think that is an overall presentation of the subject. Now, if you have any questions, I'd be very happy to do what I can to answer your specific questions.

Q: How do you dig into your subconscious?

Lester: Good question. You do it by first wanting to do it. It's very difficult when you begin, but as you do it, the more you do it, the easier it becomes. You can actually reach a place where it becomes easy. Practice will do it. By practicing bringing up subconscious thoughts, the more you do it, the more you're able to do it.

There are many aids to doing it like: "Get to the place where no one and no thing can disturb you." When someone disturbs you, and you don't know why, the thought is subconscious. Bring up the thought. By constantly trying, you will develop the habit of actually getting it up; you'll see that there's a limiting thought, an ego or selfish motivation behind it, and you'll drop it.

Q: Is just seeing the subconscious thought or motivation enough?

Lester: Just looking at it is not enough. You must consciously drop the thought or consciously will out the tendency or motivation. I'm assuming you'll want to let go of these thoughts, because they're all limiting and negative. One reason why we don't like to dig them up is that we don't like to see how awful we are. But there's nothing good or bad; there's just moving in the right direction or the wrong direction. When we move in the wrong direction, we move toward more limitation, and that's so-called bad. But everything is experiencing, and when we don't judge ourselves, we move much faster.

Q: When we don't judge ourselves?

Lester: Right. When we don't judge ourselves. Whatever comes up, so what? To get this far in your limitations, you have run the gamut of everything bad. It'll come up, but it's from past experiences.

Also, when you wake up, you'll discover that you never, ever were apart from your real Self, which is whole, perfect, complete, unlimited. All these experiences were images in your mind, just like in a night dream where you imagine everything that's going on. But while you're in a night dream, it's real to you. If someone is trying to kill you in a night dream, it's real; you're struggling for your life. But when you wake up from that dream, what do you say? "It was just a dream; it was my imagination." This waking state is exactly as real as a night dream. We're all dreaming we are physical bodies; we're dreaming the whole thing. However, in order to reach this awakened state, it is first necessary to drop a major part of your sub-conscious thinking.

Q: How do you see it when you come back after realizing it is a dream?

Lester: You see it like you now see a dream you had last night. You see it as a dream, and that's how important it remains to you. The before and after picture is simply point of view: before, you thought you were limited to a body, and all these bodies and action were so real. After, you see it as a dream, like a moving picture. When you see characters on the screen, you can lose your awareness of your-self by identifying with one of the characters on the screen, and you'll emote with him and feel unhappy.

Q: But you don't have all the desires that you had before?

Lester: You have no desires, because you wake up to the fact that you are infinite, you are the All, leaving nothing to desire. Desire limits you. "I don't have the All, therefore I must get it, and I create desires to get it." So, desire is only a limitation. When you see the full picture, you naturally lose all desire; there's nothing to desire if you are the All.

Now, practically speaking, if you choose to go along with the dream, you can act out a desire for the time being, and then act as though it's being satisfied. However, it's just an act, and you playact.

Q: How does the mind distinguish between bad and good?

Lester: By saying, "This is good and that is bad."

Q: Is that an individual thing?

Lester: Of course. What's right in one country is wrong in another; what's right to you is wrong to someone else. It's a very individualistic approach. Of course, there's some general agreement on right and wrong; we generally agree we shouldn't kill each other. So, right and wrong is a very individualistic standard. If you need a right and wrong, doing that which helps your growth is right; doing that which hinders your growth is wrong. That should be the right and wrong.

Q: Do we learn the right from experiencing?

Lester: Yes, you learn the right by doing the wrong. (Laughter.) Right? And also by experiencing the right. Unfortunately, most of us do it by actually doing the wrong thing. We learn to keep our hand out of a fire by burning it. This is what seems to prod us more than anything else–the hardships of life. We all want to get away from the misery of it, don't we? It should be the other way, that the wonderfulness of the right way should be the attractiveness of it. When you do get that far, then your growth is very fast, and you're approaching the end of the line.

Q: What did you mean by, "After you're realized, you live your life out as you preset it?" What does that mean?

Lester: We preset the behavior of this physical body before we enter it to put us through experiences that we hope to learn from.

Q: Knowing that you would attain realization this time?

Lester: No. Knowing that in past lives you subjected yourself to the law of action and reaction, cause and effect, karma (they're all the same thing), and that you want to continue that game. You did certain things when you were in a physical body before, so next time you want to set up similar things in a hope of undoing some of the things you don't like and instigating the things you do like. But you cannot change anything that the body was preset to do by you.

You're going to do exactly what you preset for that body before you came into it. There is no free will in worldly living. However, there is a free will. The free will we have is to identify with the real Being that we are, or to identify with the body. If you identify with the body, you're in trouble. So the free will is one of identity. Knowing this, it makes life much easier; you don't fight it. You aim for proper identity.

Q: The desire for bliss, would that be enough to start your search for happiness?

Lester: Sure.

Q: If one is sincere and isn't succeeding, will a Guru help them?

Lester: A realized teacher is the greatest of all help, but he can't help you any more than you will help yourself. This is most important: He cannot help you any more than you will help yourself. When you try to help yourself, he joins you and helps you to a realization that you're ready for.

Q: He helps?

Lester: He helps you get a realization that you're ready for. If you're tapped on the chest, and you get cosmic consciousness, it's because you're ready for it. Of all help, a Guru's is the greatest, because he has gone the direction, and he can help you go the same direction.

Q: How is it that when you see the dream structure of maya and you see the real Self, then all of a sudden you're caught in the dream again and you believe it? What happened?

Lester: It is possible to see your real Self and fall back into the world. Why? Because you have not let go of the subconscious thoughts, "I am this physical body; this world is real." You must go into your subconscious and make conscious all these thoughts and drop them. Or, see your Self to the degree that you see that your mind is external to you–something that you created–and then you just wipe it out.

If you can't wipe it out, and very few of us can, keep picking away at it; keep bringing up the subconscious thoughts and dropping them. Or you can make it ineffective in large chunks by willing out tendencies.

Take a particular tendency like smoking. If you've been smoking for years and years, you have thousands of little desires to smoke. The tendency is strong. However, you can say to yourself with will power, "This is ridiculous! I am through with this!" and never again have a desire for a cigarette. That's getting rid of all the thoughts of desire to smoke by willing out the tendency. That's one chunk: smoking.

Q: That's one chunk; the whole bit clear back?

Lester: Complete. I've seen many people do this on smoking with no problem. They just made that decision, and that was it!

Q: And that's how you get rid of each thing that's bothering you?

Lester: Yes. If you're jealous, look at it. If you're disgusted enough with being jealous, you say, "Finished! Done! It is gone!" and you can undo the whole thing. That's letting go of a huge piece of mind. That's letting go of many, many thoughts of jealousy that you've had in the subconscious mind. It takes some maturity to undo that tendency.

Q: And it won't come back if you really do?

Lester: Right. If you, with resolve and determination, really drop it, it's gone. You can try it on smaller things first, and when you succeed, then go to something larger. Do it on one thing. Then you can do it on two, then on all. Do that which you can do. Keep doing this every day, and it won't take you long.

Make this a way of life. Grow every day. Every incident is an opportunity for growth. Everything you're experiencing is an experience of limitation. Every annoyance you have is an excellent opportunity to transcend that. Develop the habit of digging into your subconscious for the causative thought of the annoyance and then dropping it. Daily striving assures quick arriving.

## Comments:

Are you willing for this world to be just a dream–a dream that never was? Most of us, even when we say that we are interested in freedom, spend much more time trying to prove the reality of the dream than the reality of truth or Beingness. We would rather know that we are who think we are–our limitations–than face the possibility that who we think we are is only a lie–an erroneous belief about something that never really was.

If you want to recognize the truth of who you are, you must choose to look honestly at what is actually here now. Truth is not based on memory. If you do that, you will see that what you thought you were never was, and what you are is and has always been.

## Suggestions for the week:

Allow yourself to review what you call "your past" and allow yourself to reflect on one incident at a time. It does not matter whether you label your memories as positive or negative. Both have an equal hold on your consciousness. Then ask yourself this question: "Did that really happen or was that merely a dream that never really was?" This question can allow you to wake up spontaneously to the dream nature of what we usually call reality.

If a memory seems real, as opposed to being only a dream, you can ask yourself: "Could I let go of wanting to make this memory real?" This will help you to let it go and allow it to be as it truly was–just a dream.

This process may seem difficult at first. But if you stay with it, it will get easier. Ultimately you will recognize for all time the dream nature of what we called "real" and that which is now and has always been: the one true changeless reality.

You may also want to work with the following polarities:

- That is real–That is just a dream.
- Could I allow myself to want the world to be real as much as I do? –Could I allow myself to accept the dream nature of the world as best I can?
- The world and body are real–The world and body are merely imagined.

You may also want to explore the following question: "If nothing I experience is real, then what is real?"

The next seven pages of this book are designed to help further your own exploration. You can view them as your diary of progress during the week that you are working with this session. Use the space allowed on each page to write down your gains and realizations as they happen, as well as for notes on working with the various exercises.

# Day One

# Day Two

# Day Three

# Day Four

# Day Five

# Day Six

# Day Seven

"Those who did go all the way, they did not

abandon their bodies, homes and families.

They only abandoned their former feelings of

bondage and attachment to their bodies, homes

and families, and in place of it felt free."

Lester Levenson

# Session 5

# Why Not Go All The Way?

You've been given the direction on how to go all the way. So far, none of us have taken it. We've gone to the place where life is nice, easy and comfortable; we're satisfied, not totally, but satisfied enough not to go all the way. Is it that what I promised you would be there is not enticing enough? Maybe it wasn't made promising enough? Was it? Why shouldn't you go all the way?

Q: Well, I'd like to go all the way, but it's always over the next hill. I get to this point, and it's not there; and I get to the next one, and it's not there.

Lester: Not really, because it's right where you are. Over the next hill is where it isn't. Right where you are, where the "I" of you is, is where it is.

Q: How come we don't know it?

Lester: Yes, how come? That's what I want to know.

Q: That was my question.

Lester: Yes, but what is the answer? I say it's silly not to, because once you do, you'll never, ever have a moment of unpleasantness ever again. It becomes impossible to be unhappy. What's wrong with that? Why don't we do it? I would say you don't believe it enough. You don't believe that you have no limits, you don't believe that life can be, every second, ecstatically happy. You don't believe that it can be totally effortless; you don't believe that you can do things mentally. Or is it that we keep procrastinating? I say that if we really do want to go all the way, we do it. So, again, why don't we go all the way?

Q: Well, I think in my case, I've probably hypnotized myself into believing the opposite. I've associated with the finite me all my life, in all my conscious awareness, to the degree that it is real to me.

Lester: Oh, then to you the infinite would do away with finite?

Q: Yes, because the finite is what I believe in; it's real to me. What you say about the infinite has infinite possibilities, but until I can totally accept that, it's like when you touch a light bulb and it burns you and somebody says, "Now touch it and it won't burn you." It's difficult to overcome your subconscious reaction not to touch it.

Lester: Well, let me tell you then, that the infinite includes the finite and is the basis for it. You see, you can hold onto all the finite you want when you're infinite; you don't have to lose a thing.

Q: Then I'd be glad to give it up for the infinite.

Lester: Give it up? Maybe this is what's bothering us—that we're afraid we're going to give up our bodies, that we're going to give up our families and homes. It doesn't happen that way. When those who did go all the way achieved it, they did not abandon their bodies, homes, and families. They only abandoned their former feelings of bondage and attachment to their bodies, homes, and families, and in place of it felt free.

Q: If there's happiness greater than what I've experienced in a body, to heck with this!

Lester: Well, again, you do not give up your body. Your happiness gets more intense the more you move toward total freedom, until it reaches a point where you just can't contain it anymore. Then you resolve it into a very beautiful peace that is never, ever again disturbed. And that peace is really far more delicious than the intense joy was. Then, when you choose to be active in the world, you'll never, ever lose that background peace; you will feel it all the time. And you are free to do anything in the world: you can act angry or scared, be poor or rich. You can do anything you want, but you do not disappear.

Q: It doesn't affect you?

Lester: The world can never, never touch you again, because you have imperturbable peace.

Q: I understand.

Lester: So then, why don't you come along?

Q: I am. Whenever I identify my source of income with the effort I exert in my business, I say to myself, "You're a stupid idiot. This isn't the source of my infinite supply." However, I'm not strong enough just to say, "Well, this isn't it; I'll do it the other way," because I think, "What if it doesn't work?"

Lester: You would have exactly what you had before you tried it. However, you expect it not to work if you say that.

Q: Yeah, but that's where the hang-up is. Maybe it's lack of faith—not that it hasn't worked for you, but whether it'll work for me, I am not convinced. If you could only help me, just one little infinite bit of strength that you could give me—

Lester: Oh, now wait a minute. You have the support, and I've given you many directions, any one of which would take you all the way. I could give them to you again.

Q: That's like the sign "San Francisco." I'll bet there are probably a hundred signs that point the way to San Francisco, but if I get to the sign and sit down underneath it, it would take more than just knowing where San Francisco is—and that's where I bog down.

Lester: Right, you don't take the direction; you look at it and sit down. Now, the direction: get to the place where no one and nothing can disturb you. This would have taken you all the way.

Q: Yes, but that's like going to the moon.

Lester: It is easy, if you would do it. It is your decision to be disturbed or not to be disturbed.

Q: That's quite a challenge!

Lester: Do you want more? I'll give you new ones.

Q: Yes.

Lester: Be totally selfless. Be interested only in others; have no interest in you yourself. That would take you all the way. If we would be totally selfless in our behavior—act not for ourselves but for the other ones—this would do it rapidly.

Q: I don't mean to be argumentative, but this is really a nitty-gritty.

Lester: I'll give you another one: Get to the place where you have no more desire. Keep letting go of desires until there are no more, and that's it! You don't like that one either, do you?

Q: Well, part of it. I've got a lot of things I'd like to let go of.

Lester: If anyone would carry that through until there are no more desires–and it's just letting go of them as they come up–you'd go all the way.

Q: Lester, what about the one that you and I discussed, about the mind? You see everything out there in your mind, right? So that's where everything is. So, that thing out there is just your mind. When you discover this, you change your mind, and it changes out there.

Lester: Yes, that would take you there.

Q: What about no attachments and no aversions?

Lester: That'll do it, too. That will take you all the way. But why haven't we used these things? They are not new to us.

Q: That's what I'm earnestly trying to decide for myself. This is ridiculous; all this intellectual knowledge that I've acquired and what little I've actually done with it. It's alarming. I said, "How many people have their own private Master in their family?" You've given us all this stuff, and I say, "It's my responsibility what I do with it. Why haven't I used it?"

Lester: Yes, and your private Master is you! This is important: Your private Master is you!

Q: Isn't there only one, anyway?

Lester: When you see what you really are, you'll see the Oneness and no more otherness.

Q: I try to squint, and, no matter how I do it, I still see separation.

Lester: That's the way you are approaching it, with squinty eyes. You won't look at it full view, wide open, because you are afraid you're going to disappear. So what you have to do is dig down within, pull it out, and see it. Once you see it, you'll naturally let go of that fear.

You're also afraid you're going to lose your individuality. Your individuality is something you'll never, ever lose. It's with you through eternity. The "I" that I am is never, ever lost. What happens is that we just expand it to include more and more until it includes the entire infinity. I say you're afraid of losing yourself, your body, your mind, your family, your business, and all your little things. You're subconsciously afraid you're going to lose them. If it were conscious, you'd look at it, drop it, and be free.

Q: Well, you reached me when you added those other things. The physical body attachment I don't see, but when you included my family and my business and these other things–

Lester: Do you want me to show you how attached you are to that physical body? Just imagine, don't do it, but just image throwing your body over a cliff. Can you now see your attachment to the body?

Q: Yes. But do you have to have that desire to get rid of it?

Lester: You don't get rid of it; you see what you are, and then you'll see that you are not the body, that the body is one infinitesimal part of you.

Q: Why can't I go all the way?

Lester: Because you're afraid that if you do, you're going to disappear. Does anyone feel that? That you'll disappear if you go all the way?

Q: I'm afraid I'd lose my mind. (Laughter)

Lester: You actually do lose your mind, and then you re-establish it so that you can communicate. It's far more difficult to re-establish the mind than it was originally to let go of it, because the mind itself was such a clamping down of you, you don't want to come back to it. But you will; you'll start thinking again. The only difference in the before and after picture is that now your thinking is unfree, determined by subconscious, compulsive thoughts. In the after picture, there are no more subconscious, compulsive thoughts. Every thought is totally free and without any conditioning by your tendencies and predispositions.

That leads me to another great one: Rid yourself of all your tendencies and predispositions, and you will go all the way. I have never talked much about miracles, have I? I don't feel as though I'm imposing on you now, as I used to feel, were I to talk about miracles, because, having moved up, you are more able to accept them. When I first moved to Sedona and lived by myself, most things were done by thought, and I was unaware of it. However, others began to come in, and it was because of them that I became aware of these unusual things. To me they were natural, but not to the others.

I might have told one or two of you about the teleportation incident. This one is interesting, because it involved two others—one who is following this path and another one who is not.

The first one is F- and the second one is D-, the son of T-, whom you all know. He came to Sedona from Phoenix and asked me if I would take a walk; naturally, he chose a direction uphill. We walked a mile and a half uphill, F-, D-, and I, and when we got to the end of our trip, we sat down to have our sandwiches. We had only a pint-sized canteen of water for the three of us, and we drank most of it on the way up. We had left only about an eighth of an inch of water in the bottom of this pint canteen, hardly enough for half a cup.

But the three of us were thirsty, and so I let go with the feeling "Everything is perfect!" I received the inner knowledge that the water was abundantly there. Then I asked, "Do you want a drink, F-?"

"Sure," she said. I gave F- a cupful. Then D- drank a cup, then I. We kept drinking until each one was satiated. We each had seven drinks! I curiously looked into the canteen and the same amount of water was there as originally, just about an eighth of an inch on the bottom of the canteen. We then started the downward trek for home. I was so tired that I felt as though the body would not walk anymore. I just let go, and I said, "Oh, Lord, there must be a better way!"

And the thought again came to me: "Everything is perfect." As I thought "perfect," we, the three of us, had one step up there, and the next step was down near my home, where the surroundings were similar to the place we had left so as not to make it obvious to D-.

F- caught it and said, "Lester, we teleported!"

I said, "Oh, you're crazy, F-s, you're imagining it," because D-'s mind was in a turbulence. I could tell by the frown on his face. For his sake, I had to again say, "It's your imagination, F-," and shut her up. F- knew.

Later, when she was alone without D-, I said, "What made you think we teleported?" And she laughed. She said, "Don't you remember, on the way up, D- and I were collecting rocks, and in several places we put them on the left side of the road on the way up (the road was cut into the side of the hill). I wanted to pick up those rocks on the way back, but we by-passed all of those places.

Now, to do these things, it takes a mere effortless thought: you surrender, let go, and have a thought with no effort, no drive. It's the easiest thought you could have. And then it happens.

During the early days in Sedona, I was living this way, unaware of it. To me, it was natural. Whatever I thought, I expected. It seemed natural, just the way everyone thinks he lives naturally. It is really the natural way, and it is meant for us to live that way. Although, if we did, we wouldn't fit very well into our present society, would we? So, if you want to stay in communication, you go the way of people. Miracles are just this dream world effected immediately.

And miracles don't necessarily mean spiritual development, because the majority of people in the universe use these things. They use them on other planets where they're not necessarily more spiritually advanced than we. It is their natural way of life. But the easier way to live is purely mentally–mentally do everything. You people should be able to do all this.

Why not go all the way and have nature serve you? Why do you do things the harder way? I think it's because you're afraid you're going to disappear. I'm saying to you, "Look, I have been through these things. And I still have a body here. I didn't disappear."

Q: Can you demonstrate your infinity for me, too?

Lester: You must demonstrate your own. You have had ample

witnessing of these unusual things. If I do it for you, that would mean you can't do it. I just finished saying that you can do it! It's surrendering, then mere effortless thinking! You have the feeling that it is not I, but the Father who worketh through me. I can go on and on. I'm trying to entice you.

When I moved into the mobile home on my grounds, a girl, now living here in Laguna Beach, asked me, "How often do you fill that butane bottle?" (It was a five-gallon bottle.) I said, "Every month." Then I remembered it had been eight months since I had last filled it. Becoming aware of it, I let go of it.

When I was trying to show F- how to conserve water, I let her take charge of and keep filled my fifty-five-gallon water drum along-side my mobile home. It took care of all my needs, including a shower every morning. The reason why I wanted her to take care of it was that I wanted to show her that you can live on very little water. But I lost track of time, and when I brought it to her attention, she laughed. It had been four months since she had filled it last. I kept using the water, and the tank wouldn't empty out! When we opened it and looked, it was still full after using it for four months. It never would have emptied out if I had not let go of it.

Q: "Had not let go of it." What do you mean?

Lester: Let go of it by letting it be "normal."

Q: You thought again of it as being a limited thing?

Lester: No, I let it be as usual, or as is normal to people. I want to remain in communication with people, and I choose to live like people live, because if I live in an unusual way, I'm out of communication. It even scares people.

Q: This wouldn't scare anybody.

Lester: I know by experience that it scares people. When it first came to me while I was living in New York City, some people wouldn't come near me because of these things happening. What's wrong with this way of life? Why won't you take it? It is yours for the taking. I hope to allure you by making it so tempting that you will go all the way. Look at the difficulties you go through to make a living. Ask yourself, "Why don't I go all the way?" Why don't I take things directly, just for the thought of them? Why don't I express my total freedom?" And maybe the answer will come up, and you'll see what you're doing to hold yourself down.

Q: One reason is that we are so used to being hamstrung that we don't realize that we can get out of it. I was just thinking of the motel, of getting it sold, and then I thought, "Do I really want to leave it?" And I know I upset it every time.

Lester: That's true, and that is why I'm telling you of the easy way. Your habit of thought runs you the hard way. One way to undo all habits of thought, which are in the subconscious mind, is to see that you are not the mind, and you will scorch it.

Q: Tell us a little more about scorching this mind, which I have found out is most important.

Lester: I see you've gotten a realization just recently.

Q: That's right.

Lester: And yet, you didn't carry through on it. With that realization, you should have continued and said, "I can do it; I am infinite!" With that infinite power, you just pass your figurative hand over the mind and it's finished. It's just a mental wipe-out that you do, and that's it. You know how long it takes ? Less than that (finger snap)! Less than a second. When you get your full realization, it's instantaneous. Before that, you play around, dropping a little bit at a time. This goes on and on, year in and year out, until you decide to let go of the whole thing. Then you've got full realization. It really comes instantaneously when it comes. You will it. Will is your power. You turn on your will so strongly that you just undo the whole mind, and you are totally free.

Q: It just doesn't make any sense at all. It's just as though you're handing me all the money in the world and saying, "Here!" and I'm sitting and saying, "Why don't I take it?"

Lester: Yes, why don't you?

Q: What's wrong with me?

Lester: What is? That's the big question. What is wrong? I know you think that this is possible, otherwise you would not have listened all this time.

Q: It's the intellect that's in the way.

Lester: That is it. Why not wipe it out? The intellect is the mind. We have to see we're not the mind, and that it is external to us, and then just make it ineffective. Just like that; that's the way you'll do it.

Q: You said something the other night, Lester, which was a help to me and that was, "I am going to put Lester to bed." So, I've said this to myself several times. "I am going to have him do so and so." And he's been doing so and so.

Lester: I always think that way. I'll send Lester and this body around and make it appear to be doing things. After I got the realization that I am not the body, it was years before I could use the word "I." People would laugh at me, because I'd talk about Lester. I would talk about "him," and sometimes I would say, "It, Lester," or, "Lester, he." I couldn't say "I" even though I was being corrected. Why? I was not this body. I could talk about this body, but it was so obvious and glaring that I was not this body that I couldn't say I was this thing, any more than you could say you were your car. Because you are carrying yourself around in a car, would you call yourself the car? In the same way, you'll look at this body. (This body is a carcase, a carcass.) I say you're silly to not take the All.

Q: I think there's a stronger word than silly.

Lester: Yes, it's really stupid. He led me to say it. (Laughter.) It's so stupid not to go through life with everything you want, with nothing but extreme joy, peace, and loveliness every moment when that is your inherent state. It takes no effort to be what you are. It does take extreme effort to be what you are not: a body with trouble, sicknesses, and needing this and needing that. It takes effort to be what you're not, but to be what you are takes as much effort as you women would need to be a female and as much effort as you men would need to be a male. It takes no effort to be what you are. And yet you persist in using effort to be what you are not. It's really stupid!

Q: Well, I persist in using effort to try to be what you say I am. I keep working at this thing of being effortless. Does that make sense?

Lester: No, does it?

Q: Not to me.

Lester: Right. There's something wrong there.

Q: What did I say?

Lester: You're using effort in trying to make yourself effortless—that's impossible! It's a contradiction. You've got to stop using effort. You've got to let go and let be. That's what is meant by "Let go and let God." You are it, you're the god—let go and let your Self be. However, it seems to take much effort, because you are using tremendous effort to hold onto and maintain your non-self, your ego, and there is where your effort is. It takes no effort to be what you are—the Self.

Q: If I could arrive at the dreamer instead of the dream, then I'd have it made. And that's why I've been thinking, "This is a dream? Who's dream is this?"

Lester: Right! Discover the dreamer. To make it more intimate: I, the infinite Being, am dreaming that I am a limited body. While you are in a night dream, and you think you are a limited body in that night dream, it persists so long as you don't wake up. It's the same thing with this waking state. We're dreaming we're limited bodies. We have to wake up to the fact that we are infinite. We have to stop thinking that we're limited bodies, that's all. Stop thinking. Let go. Let be. Surrender is the word.

If we would surrender this moment, that would be it. Not I, but thou. Not my will, but Thy will. This is surrender. We could do that right now and that would be it. But no, we've got to be a busy ego-body, doing something. We must be a doer.

Q: Some of the people at the motel were discussing robots. Actually, I guess we could consider the body a robot. We're using this physical body, and when we're through with it, we drop the physical body, but what we have is still there.

Lester: That's an excellent way to look upon the body. All right, now I'll tell you something more. If you were really convinced of what I've said so far, you'd go home. You'd forget everything else, and you'd sit down until you saw this, because this would give you everything, just for the thought. If you were really convinced, you'd go home determined to sit until you see this; and if you did that, you'd see it! Just like Buddha did, when he left his throne and sat under a tree, determined not to leave until he saw the answer; and he saw the answer.

Q: Well, I think one thing that may be bogging some of us down, and I know to a certain extent it has to me, is that I have felt for a long time that I had to take something piecemeal and get each thing out of my system. Now, I'm finally beginning to realize that if I get above it, then none of it makes any difference.

Lester: Yes. We all start that way by undoing single things at first. It begins to show us our mastership. Then we master our tendencies or predispositions. This undoes all the numerous multitudes of thoughts that made up that tendency or predisposition. You should not keep undoing these single things piecemeal. That was all right for the beginning; you don't need it anymore. Drop a tendency or predisposition, and you drop the millions of subconscious thoughts underlying it.

Q: When you first started to tell us that there's nobody out there but you, some of us just couldn't understand that, me included. I have discovered why there's nobody out there but me: because it is I who creates that out there, and it is in me.

Lester: Yes, that's true!

Q: So, I really know. I had a realization that was as clear as crystal.

Lester: Okay, why not clean up that "out there" until you do not waiver from seeing it all as in you?

Q: That's what I'm doing now.

Lester: You don't take enough time at it.

Q: That's true.

Lester: It should be all the time, regardless of what you're doing. While you're driving, talking to people, you can remain with it, and you would if you wanted it that much. If you really get with it, the joy of doing it is so great that you won't let go until you go all the way. It becomes the only thing you want. You begin to see the light, and then nothing in this world can interest you more than it. You just stay with it and you ride it all the way. Misery starts you in the direction, gets you to reverse your wrong direction. Then the desire for the wonderfulness of it takes you all the way to the top.

Q: Then you know you can play any game you want, because that mind is under your control.

Lester: Yes. However, the game played is after reaching the top is usually the same game for everyone, although it will express differently; it's the game of helping others, which is really a great game.

Q: It becomes an interesting game.

Lester: It's the nicest game there is; it's the most rewarding game there is.

Q: What you are teaching me is really helping me.

Lester: That which I'm offering you is more than a million dollars. What I'm offering is the whole universe. If you wanted gold, you could pile it up by the tons. Of course, when you can create unlimited tons of gold, do you want to pile it up? No, you take only that which you can use.

Q: Of all the different ways that you've offered, it seems like there ought to be one that I could be successful with.

Lester: Take any one of my many sayings and, if you carry it out until the end, that would be it. Take the good one mentioned before: Get to the place where no one and nothing can disturb you. Every time you are disturbed, look for the ego-motivation wherein you wanted it to be other than it was. On recognizing it, say, "Oh, I see," and let go of your ego-motivation of wanting it to be the way you want it to be. Every reaction or tendency is based on a selfish thing. We wanted it to be the way we wanted it to be. Keep dropping these reactive tendencies. Every time a reaction comes, look at it; see the selfish ego-motivation and drop it. You'll soon reach a place where there is no more, and you're there–all the way.

Q: Every time you feel offended or jealous or angry or hurt or anything like that, that's your ego, and that's your mind.

Lester: Right. Rid yourself of all your feelings, and you will go all the way. So, have we gained anything new?

Q: You have presented us with more of a challenge to understand what you're saying; you make it sound so darn easy, and it affronts me to think that anything that easy could elude me.

Lester: When you do it, it is easy. When you don't do it, it's impossible. That's the way it really is. When you do it, it's easy. When you don't do it, it's impossible.

Q: Oh, lord, wait a minute. When you do it, it's easy. When you don't do it, it's impossible.

Lester: It takes no effort to be what you really are: infinite. It takes tremendous effort to be extremely limited as you now choose to be. I feel as though I've given what I could on going all the way. If there's any further question, I'll be happy to do what I can to answer it. If not, this is it.

Q: I keep looking at you, and I see that there's hope. If you've made it, somebody has. It isn't impossible, and I can do it.

Lester: Yes, do it. Go all the way. Everyone was moving rapidly upward and then leveled off; some came down just a little bit and leveled off there. If you don't use what you've seen, you'll lose it. You have got to keep using it, otherwise the remaining subconscious habits will overwhelm you, and you will lose your direction.

Q: When we go all the way, we still go on doing the same things: we still go on laughing, we still go to the ballet, do all these things. There's nothing denied.

Lester: Yes. The only difference is that you're free to do or not to do whatever you want; you're no longer compelled in any direction whatsoever. I strongly recommend taking time out for thinking on these things every day, twice a day. In the morning before going to work and at night before going to bed. Never should a day go by without doing this. Get with it, totally in a quiet spot, until it sucks you in more and more, until you let go of the world pull. Getting quiet enough, the infinite part of you just takes over, and you go all the way. You reach a place where you feel helpless, because it's effortless. Keep that up, and you'll effortlessly be sucked right into your infinity.

Q: Well, I know. Sometimes it seems that I'm getting so tall.

Lester: There's a sense of surrender in that.

Q: There's that famous statement of yours: Let go and let God. It finally struck me that that means let go of your mind and let God.

Lester: Yes, another way to say that is, "Surrender." Even if you surrender to a mountain, you will get it, because surrender is "Not my will."

Q: Ego, mind, and will are all the same thing. So, if you let it, that means letting go of your mind, ego, and all the other things.

Lester: Yes.

Q: Sometimes when something happens, I can be very irritated, but then I catch myself giggling to myself while I'm doing it. It really isn't affecting me.

Lester: Yes, get free, and then you may act irritated.

Q: So you can act any part? And you're aware of the fact that you're an actor?

Lester: Right. Go all the way and there is only fun.

Q: You can even keep your humor, too?

Lester: Right. But the motivation for the humor is to make others happy, not for ego-approval. That's the difference.

When I say you people leveled off and are on a plateau, it's not exactly correct. You leveled off into a slow, gradual, upward direction. It could be much faster, even immediate, rather than a slow, gradual, upward trend. Go all the way, and then life from that point on is just a ball. You don't have to work. If you want to, you can. You can always be successful—or you can even choose to be unsuccessful, just to make a game out of it. If you can succeed in failing, you can also succeed in succeeding.

Q: Would helping others really be a fast way?

Lester: Not so if your purpose is ego-motivated. However, when you live only for others, it's a very fast way. Paradoxically, the most selfish thing you can do is to be totally selfless. When we are totally selfless, we have the All, the infinity. It's a seeming paradox.

Q: That's it. You offer me the All!

Lester: Yes. We've all had glimpses of it. The thing to do is to establish that permanently, for all time. So, again I say, take time out every day and effect it. Go all the way. You've got infinite power behind you; there's nothing to stop you but you. Make it part of your every day life, and stay with it until it's established for all time. You can do it!

## Comments:

What do you believe you must give up in order to be free? If we were honest with ourselves, most of us would have quite a long list. But what if what Lester said is correct? There is no giving up on the path to freedom; there is only a taking on of more and more until you recognize you are the All. You can have a direct experience of being the All if you will it or are completely open to it. As Lester used to say, "Try it, you'll like it."

## Suggestions for the week:

Most of us do not let ourselves discover our true nature because of fear. But there is a secret about fear. Once you learn it, you can use it to help you let go of all fear, including whatever fear you have about recognizing your true nature—your freedom. Here it is: Anything that we are afraid of we subconsciously want to happen—and eventually it does.

We may see or hear about something that has happened to someone else. Or we may experience something directly that we don't like. We want to avoid these things. So we think, "I hope this does not happen to me," or, "I hope this never happens again." But, because the mind thinks and creates in pictures, it is not able to visualize a negation. By holding a picture in our minds of what we fear happening, we create it.

You can use the above information to let go of any fear including the fears associated with being fully awake. Ask yourself: "What am I afraid will happen if I wake up or I am totally free?" No matter how you respond to that question, ask yourself: "Could I let go of wanting that to happen?" As you do, you will be letting go of your artificial obstacles to freedom and will feel more and more open to waking up to your true nature.

You may also want to explore the following polarities:
• There is something to fear–There is nothing to fear.
• I can't be totally free–I can be totally free.
• Freedom is impossible–Freedom is easy.
• I can go free–I am freedom itself.

The next seven pages of this book are designed to help further your own exploration. You can view them as your diary of progress during the week that you are working with this session. Use the space allowed on each page to write down your gains and realizations as they happen, as well as for notes on working with the various exercises.

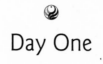

# Day One

# Day Two

# Day Three

# Day Four

# Day Five

# Day Six

# Day Seven

"Look away from the body.

Look away from the mind.

Look toward the Beingness that you are

and never stop until you fully discover

that Thou Art That!"

Lester Levenson

# Session 6

# Thou Art That

Everyone is aware of the infinite Being that he is. Are you aware of the "I" that you are? The word "I" is the Beingness part of you. But it's only the Beingness part. If you experience "I am," that's it. That part of you is infinite, and you are experiencing it all the time. There's no time when you are not experiencing it–otherwise you'd go out of existence. However, you override it and hide it from yourself by saying, "I am a body." And what you're doing is saying, "I, the infinite Being, am this body."

So, if you use the word "I," you're talking of the infinite Being that you are. Every time you say, "I am something," you're saying, "I, the infinite Being, am a limited something." And being infinite, it allows you to assume limitation as much as you want. That's why you can do such a good job of limiting yourself. Does that make sense?

Q: Yes.

Lester: We can drive ourselves into such extreme limitation that we think we are a victim of our environment and subject to it. And it is an infinite Being doing that!

Q: Why do we not realize our unlimited Being?

Lester: We have the conviction that we can't do it. If we were not convinced that we couldn't do it, we could do it quickly, even in a moment. How long should it take one with all knowledge, all power to recognize that he is all knowledge, all power? No time! And each one of us is that all-powerful, all-knowing individual. It seems so hard, almost impossible, only because we won't do it. That's why it's so difficult, because we won't do it! You hold the concept that you are a body rather than that you are an infinite, unlimited Being. As long as you hold to that concept, you're stuck with it. You don't look at the other, the opposite side of you, which is unlimited.

Q: Well then, could you say that the only thing between us and realization is a thought, really?

Lester: Yes, that's it. It is a thought that is the culmination of much thought. If you would just examine how your thoughts flow after I tell you that you are unlimited, you would discover that immediately you dive right into the thoughts of being a limited body.

When I say that each one of you is infinite, unlimited–right now–at that moment you get a feel of it. Are you aware of the feeling that you get as I say it? Right now, everyone here is infinite, unlimited, omnipotent, omniscient, omnipresent. When I say that to you, for that instant you feel it; but the next moment you think you are the body and immediately take your full attention off what you really want and put it on the concept of being only the body with all its affiliations.

All right, now that you have heard this, why don't you stop doing this to yourselves? (Interruption: Two people arrive and enter the room, causing much conversation.) You have an example right now of what I've been talking about. Can you see what just happened? If what I said had been held onto, you would not have been distracted by the newcomers; the people would have come in and quietly sat down, and nothing would have been said. But we're so interested in bodies that we immediately gravitate toward them. This is the problem, our persistence in being bodies. Every moment we hold that, we are limited bodies.

What you need to do is stop doing just that. Will you do it? If you do, you will see the infinite Being that you are. It's really simple but seems extremely difficult. Not only difficult but impossible, doesn't it? It is, only because we just don't do it, and that makes it impossible. We've heard these things again and again and again. But what use is it listening to this if we don't do it? And, as I said, being infinite, there isn't anyone here who couldn't be the infinite Being he is right here and now, if only he would do it.

So, what you need to do is to get with yourself, look at yourself, and do it. And it's that simple. How many of you women go about every day trying to discover that you're a female? None. Who of you men go about every day trying to discover that you are a male? Why don't you? Why don't you people want to be told that? Because you accept it without any doubt whatsoever. But you do not accept that you are infinite. Why not? Why play the game of limitation and be miserable? Why? I'm asking you the questions now instead of you asking me.

You believe you're infinite. Why don't you be what you are, instead of this constant trying to be the limited body? The body is a very cramped thing to be, and it hurts, lifetime in and lifetime out. Why do you insist on being so cramped and incapacitated, as everyone is if one is a physical body? Compared to what one really is–infinite, unlimited and totally free–it is ridiculous, isn't it? Maybe someone might want to answer the question, "Why don't you be what you are: infinite?"

Q: What does it feel like to be infinite?

Lester: Absolutely no limitation in any direction whatsoever. No limitations: total freedom from everything, needing no food, no oxygen, no job. Instantly materializing anything you want. Being anywhere in the universe. Being as tall as you want, or the size of an atom. Being at perfect peace and contentment. Being in the most delightful state possible.

Q: What happens to this body when that happens?

Lester: To really know that you should experience what you are. Otherwise, the reality of the body can't be understood. When you see what you are, only then do you know what the body is. It turns out to be a thought, a thought just like in a night dream when you dreamed about being a body in a situation. And when you awoke, you said, "Oh, my gosh, that was all in my mind."

The same thing happens to this body when you wake up from this dream called the waking state. You see the body, but you know it to be the dream nature that it is. Do you see how much you're concerned about the body? And this point I make: Be as concerned about your infinite Being as you are about your body; if you are, you will discover that you are infinite.

Q: What I really meant was, when you are away doing these things, how does this body function?

Lester: Automatically. However, you can't be away from the "I" that you are. You're right where your "I" is. When you say "I," that's where you are. You can't get away from it, ever. The individuality never leaves you, and you never leave it. The "I" that you are always is. It's eternal. That's the real Being that you are.

All right now, if you will be that "I," and only that "I," then everything will turn out to be like a dream. And when you see it full, a dream that never really was, it's the same as when you wake up from a nightmare. A good allusion to what we are going through now is the nightmare. As long as you remain in it, it's a horrible thing, and it's very real. It only becomes unreal to you after you awaken. Right? The exact same thing happens to this waking state dream when we wake up from it. We first say, "Oh, my gosh, it was all a dream," and then we add, "That never really was."

And that's what happens to your body. You then see it as a dream body. Your body will change, but you never will change. You don't disappear; you don't lose anything. You just take on more and more until you see yourself first, as every Being, as every body, and then as every atom in the universe. There's no reason to fear losing your body or losing anything. You gain more and more until you become infinite. Yet, most of us are fearful lest we're going to lose our body and be nothing. That's a serious error. You could be a hundred bodies!

Q: If you think of the body in terms of Beingness—

Lester: If you do, you're committing a gross crime against the word "Beingness." Beingness is the infinity that you are. Your Beingness is infinite. Your being a body is an extreme limitation in your Beingness.

Q: We think of body in terms of limitation; that's the ordinary concept of body.

Lester: Right, which means we have to let go of the concept: The body is I. As long as we hold that, we are holding the concept: I am an extreme limitation, a physical body. Any slight maladjustment in it, and it dies. And everyone knows that it does, sooner or later. What's this great thing called a body? It's a very disposable thing, and everyone knows that sooner or later he will dispose of it, right? But gosh, how we hold onto this limitation! And keep ourselves in extreme confinement! We are like a bird in a cage, with the door open, refusing to fly free!

Q: Well, this sense of Beingness, infinite Beingness, is far more concrete than our present sense of body, is it not?

Lester: It should be. This is what, in effect, I'm saying. If you just hold onto your sense of Beingness and just hold that, and not add "This body is I," just hold onto your Beingness only—and hold it and hold it—you'll be letting go of the feeling that the body is I. And you'll get an insight into this Beingness, as to what it is, and then you will remain in it. Then your Beingness is very concrete to you, and your body is like a dream body. When you are only Beingness, you recognize that your Beingness is all Beingness. I say that everyone here is, right now, that infinite Beingness. And the infinite part of you is the "I," the Beingness of the "I," the, "I am." And if you would hold that, that would become real and concrete to you, and all the limitation, misery, and trouble of the body would automatically be gone.

Q: I've had a few glimpses of that, but holding it is a different thing.

Lester: The reason why you don't hold it is because you are holding onto the body being you.

Q: The thing is that this Beingness cannot be conceived of with the mind, can it?

Lester: Right. However, you don't have to conceive of it if you are it. Do you have to conceive of being a male? Just only be it.

Q: But this metamorphosis, this change that must take place within the individual, requires some intellectualization at first?

Lester: The intellect directs you toward looking away from what you are not and looking at what you are. In that sense, you're right. We ask, "What am I?" and that's intellectual. However, the answer is an experience.

Q: Now this is what I was getting at. When does this intellectualization of the infinite stop, and you realize it as it is?

Lester: When your thinking quiets enough, you then see what you are, and it becomes real to you.

Q: But you're not conscious of that transition?

Lester: You're conscious of letting go of the concepts of limitation. Discovering the infinite Being that you are is no transition, because you are that now; you always have been and always will be that. So there can't be any transition there. It's the letting go of the thoughts of limitation that is a transition.

Q: Isn't it difficult for one to think of his inner Being as infinite?

Lester: In your thinking, it's impossible. You can only experience it.

Q: And yet it's real; you do come into it. There's no doubt about it.

Lester: Yes, sooner or later. When you get so fed up with torturing yourself, you then let go of all the nonsense, and you'll be what you really are–infinite. Now, most people on earth will take millions of years to do this, and you can see why. When we take into account all people, you're very advanced. And look how much you are holding onto being only that body! Your questions and talk relate mostly to the body, its transition, and what happens to the body. I'm hoping to provoke you into letting go of identifying with the body, by telling you it's impossible to be infinite, because you insist upon being the body. And so long as you persist in being the body, it is impossible. You're stuck. And you could remain this way for millions of years. Have you ever accepted the concept that you have no limitations?

Q: I've accepted the idea intellectually, but obviously not in practice.

Lester: Yes, and because you believe you are a body, it is impossible to be infinite. These bodies are very frail things, and they don't last very long, either. And we insist and persist in being the body. Now any time anyone decides—really decides—not to be it, then he will allow himself to see his infinite Beingness.

What do we do twenty-four hours a day? We cater to the body; we think we are it! We wake it up in the morning, we wash it, we dress it, we beautify it. We send it off to work so it can earn some money, so that we can put some other life (food) into it so it can rot (digest) that life inside so that it can persist. And then we go home, and we park it for the evening. It is such a wonderful life that we have to escape from it; every night we have to go unconscious, that is, go to sleep. And this we repeat day in and day out, life in and life out, until we decide that we are not the body, that we are more than the body, that we are infinite Beingness. It is really simple. The difficulty of it is the holding onto wanting to be the body. We are constantly saying, "I am the body; I am not infinite." And, of course, we can't feel the unlimited joy or happiness that we're seeking by cramping ourselves into a little body that's frail and perishable.

Q: What do you mean when you say we have such a wonderful life that we have to go unconscious?

Lester: This life that we think is so great, we cannot take twenty-four hours a day. For about eight hours every day, we have to escape it through the unconscious state of being asleep.

Q: While asleep, where am I? Why can't I remember?

Lester: Because you believe you can't. The reason is that you don't want to, because, unless you relate to the physical body and world, you believe you are a void. However, notice the fact that, although you drop the physical body and world in sleep, you still exist, don't you? Sleep is an escape from this wonderful world of ours. As we go up into higher states of Beingness, we all reach a place where we don't sleep anymore. When we do not dislike the world, there's no need to go to sleep. I want to point out how wonderful this world is. How wonderful is it if we have to escape from it every night? So, let go of it and be what you are. Be infinite. Stop looking at the world and look at the "I that I am," and keep your attention on the "I that I am" until you see it fully, and you'll drop being only a physical body with all the limitation associated with it.

Q: We keep imagining that this little limited life brings us happiness, and that helps keep us bound, doesn't it?

Lester: Yes, so why do it? Everyone is seeking the infinite Being that he is. You call it happiness, happiness with no sorrow. It is your Self, your Beingness. Why not just be it? Why don't you do it?

Q: Well, I guess we don't want it badly enough; we're afraid to go all out.

Lester: That's it, you don't want it enough. You want to be the limited body with all its adjuncts of limitation—sickness, trouble, and finally death. Ridiculous, isn't it?

Q: Actually, if this were the most important thing in your life, it wouldn't take long to become that. But we all have our side tracks that keep us going in all directions.

Lester: That's it. We really don't want this knowledge of our unlimited state, right? Therefore, our attention is in the other directions.

Q: It's unlimited, we know this intellectually, but do you think we have a resistance, not knowing exactly what is there for us?

Lester: Yes, and no. You know you're infinite, and you're seeking it. In your every act, every day, you're seeking this infinite Being that you are. You call it happiness. If you would trace happiness down to its source, you would discover that there is no happiness in external things or people. Happiness is something you experience within. And it's there all the time if you just don't cut it off by making it dependent on someone liking you, or on your getting gold.

Once I say, "In order for my inner happiness to be, I must have gold," I cut off that happiness unless I get gold. So we're cutting off that unlimited happiness and saying it's in the world, in tiny bits, while all the time it's unlimited right within us, not out there in the world. But, as you said, we're so convinced that it's in the world that our attention is in directions other than on the infinite Being that we are. If we really wanted to see this infinite Being that we are, our attention would be there all the time.

Q: And we could be that right at that moment!

Lester: Right. At that moment, or soon, or in a month or two. But

I say you are condemned to millions of years of misery if you persist in being the body.

Q: If one experiences very intense misery where everything seems to be cut off, an awakening can come out of this sometimes, can't it?

Lester: Oh yes. That's the way we usually do it. When we are in the direction of limitation, we keep making ourselves more and more limited until we go to extremes and think we are in danger of becoming incapacitated with something severe, with sickness or death. Then, with our determination, which everyone has, we say, "To hell with this!" and we go in the right direction.

However, we could and should go in the right direction because of the wonderfulness of it.

Q: I think the tendency often is to try to contact the infinite and then use it to make this finite life comfortable, pleasant, prosperous, and things like that.

Lester: Right. We try to contact our unlimited power and then use it to make a better body and world. We can make the body and world better, but we cannot achieve sustained happiness, because being subject to this body and world is being subject to limitation and non-freedom.

Q: But getting rid of your body isn't going to help much, though, is it?

Lester: I'm not suggesting you do. Until you can consciously leave your body, if you forcibly got rid of your body, you would just come back again through the womb and wait twenty years while growing up before starting again to learn that you're not the body. So, forcibly dropping the body would be a very wrong thing to do. But to show you how much you think you are the body, just ask yourself how close could you come to throwing your body out on the highway and letting cars run over it. This will show you how convinced you are that your body is you.

Q: Is it our unconscious mind that prevents us from being our infinity?

Lester: It's you, making your thoughts unconscious. I say it's you; it's not your mind. Or, if you want to argue it, show me this mind you are talking about. Where is it? And how is it holding you back? Does it have a life other than you? Is it other than you? What is this thing? You're preventing yourself, whether via the mind, the body, anything. You are doing it. It's important that you take full responsibility, because, if you don't, you will never get out of this trap.

Q: I understand that it is something that we have created ourselves, but it has reached such a proportion!

Lester: Not it, it is you who have reached such a proportion. So long as you blame something else, you'll never get out of it. You're doing it. Can't you see that you cannot undo your limitation as long as you'll not take responsibility for it? No matter what you call it, whether you call it mind, or body, you are doing it.

Q: I am taking responsibility for it, because I'm trying to do something about it.

Lester: Okay. As long as you say, "I'm taking responsibility," that's all right. But when you say, "It is the mind," you are not taking responsibility for it. Then the mind is responsible, not you. Do you see that?

Q: Well, I'm responsible for it; it's my creation.

Lester: Right. Whose mind is it? It's yours.

Q: But, still, it has become a sort of Frankenstein's monster that's gotten out of hand. And isn't that what stands in the way?

Lester: No, you do. As long as you think it's something other than you, you have no chance. As you speak now, you are convinced that the mind is doing it, and not you.

Q: So we make the mistake that the mind is going to see, and the mind will never see it.

Lester: Right!

Q: And we're so conditioned to function as mind that that seems to be the only tool we know we have, and so we're using the wrong tool.

Lester: Right.

Q: So, what we need to do is just throw the tool out.

Lester: Right. Then what's left over is the infinite you. Throw the tool out. It takes no tools to be what you are!

Q: That's the mistake; we keep trying to do it with the mind, because that's the only thing we're familiar with.

Lester: It's not the only thing you're familiar with; you are also familiar with the "I" that you are. Just the word "I," and that's you, that's not your mind. You have the mind. You are always experiencing this infinite Being that you are, and it's the "I." You lose sight of this infinite "I" by identifying the mind and body as you. Let go of identifying with your body and mind, and what is right there in the pure "I" is an infinite Being–you. Simple enough?

Q: You say the "I" has been for billions of years. Is the "I" always the same?

Lester: The "I" that you really are is always the same: changeless, eternal, and perfect.

Q: It has always been the way it is, and the way it will be?

Lester: It has always been that way: perfect, changeless, immortal. And that's why we have the tendency to think of the body that way. We try to make it perfect and immortal, even though we know we can't.

Q: Does the body serve a purpose?

Lester: Yes, it hurts; it confines. This serves to redirect you back to seeing that you are infinite. The purpose of having the body is to help you learn that you have no limitation. So, you conjured up the extreme limitation called the physical body in order to learn that you have no limitation. That body is going to hurt more and more the more you think that you are it, until someday you say, "The heck with it!" Then, with full determination to see what you really are, you suddenly awaken to what has always been–that you are infinite.

Q: Has the "I" always used the body?

Lester: No, the "I" never used the body. The "I" is changeless and perfect. The "I" imagined, dreamed, it used the body. It's an illusion; it's a dream, but while you're in the dream, it seems real. Wake up out of this dream. See what you are. That is the thing to do. Notice how much you ask me questions about the body. Are you aware of that?

Q: In order, I guess, to define it.

Lester: No, you are trying to express your infinity in terms of this extreme limitation. And this is why you're stuck. Reverse it. Let go of the body. Put all your attention on the infinite "I" that you are, and only then will you have a possibility of seeing the infinite "I" that you are. You must let go of the concept of that body being you.

Q: Pain is a great awakener, then, isn't it?

Lester: Yes. However, we're not aware of how much pain there is, because we have accustomed ourselves to it and made ourselves immune to the real amount. Because we're infinite Beings, and we're trying to be this limited body. It's very painful. And when you awaken from this dream, you'll see how much pain there was. It's almost infinite pain compared to what you really are, which is infinite joy. I'm emphasizing that you should be not the body and be not the mind, but just be.

Q: In meditation, doesn't one use the mind to a certain extent?

Lester: Yes, however meditation is used for quieting the mind. You use the mind to quiet the mind. When the mind is quiet enough, this infinite Being that you are becomes obvious. That is the whole purpose of meditation. If anyone gets his mind quiet enough, he cannot help but see this infinite Being that he is, because it's only the thoughts that cover it. And the mind is nothing but thoughts. So, meditation is used to get the mind quieter, until you get it so quiet that you see your Self, your real Self.

Q: Would directing the thought toward the infinite be a step toward getting there?

Lester: Yes. However, it is another thought.

Q: It's another thought, but some thoughts are more God-revealing than others, are they not?

Lester: No thought can reveal God. Every thought hides or covers

God, your Self. Every thought is a chain; nice thoughts are golden chains. A golden chain will keep you imprisoned just as much as an iron chain. You must undo all thinking. Get the mind quiet, and then quiet enough so the infinite Being that you are is self-obvious. It's there all the time; the thoughts are the noise that's covering it. However, if you must have thoughts, a thought in the direction of God is much better than a thought in other directions, as it points you toward God.

Q: But if the infinite is non-mind, how can you speak of it as infinite, because infinite is a mental concept?

Lester: No. No mental thought can be infinite. Every thought is a limitation.

Q: Then how can you know that you are infinite? How can you vocalize it?

Lester: You cannot mentally conceive of infinity, nor can you vocalize it. That is impossible. Try it when you're home. It's impossible to conceive of unlimitedness.

Q: Well, it's an experience.

Lester: Right, it's not a thought; it's an experience, an experience of being infinite. The mind can allude to it but cannot describe it. Any description is necessarily a limitation.

Q: Where does the mind begin, and where does the mind end?

Where does God begin, and where does God end? And where does the infinite begin, and where does the infinite end?

Lester: God, the infinite, the Self, has no beginning and no end. The mind has a beginning when you create it. It has an end when you let it go.

Q: It seems to be a painful struggle to let it go.

Lester: You're holding onto it while trying to let go of it. The holding onto it is the pain. Why don't you just be what you are? Why question me on the opposite side, on the struggle? Why do you talk about it? Because you're interested in it, and you would like me to relate the infinite to it.

Q: Well then, if, when you think, you just know who is thinking—that takes care of it?

Lester: Right! Discover who the thinker is, and you'll have the answer. When you discover who the one is that has the mind and has the body and does the thinking, you discover the real you, an infinite Being. So, look away from the body! Look away from the mind, and look toward the Beingness that you are and never stop until you fully discover that thou art that!

Comments:

A quote from this session is a key for your awakening: "God, the infinite, the Self, has no beginning and no end. The mind has a beginning when you create it. It has an end when you let it go." We actually recreate the illusion of the mind every day after we wake up and every time we refer to "I" as anything but the infinite Being that we are. But the mind does not ever exist. It only appears to exist when we refer to it as previously mentioned. We also let the mind go between our days in order to sleep. And we let go of the mind whenever we are fully present and engaged with what is now without saying this is "me" or "this is mine."

So you are picking up and recreating the illusion of mind all the time. Yet it is never ever real.

## Suggestions for the week:

Allow yourself to become aware of how you are recreating the illusion of "me" or of "mind." As you catch yourself appearing to create limitation, switch your attention to becoming aware of that which never changes and is always present as Beingness. "I" all alone. You can do this throughout your day.

It is especially helpful when you awaken first thing in the morning to notice that all there is is the "I." After we awaken, we attach the "I" to person, place, or thing. You can also become aware of how you automatically let go of "me" or "mind" when you fall asleep. In fact, if you did not let it go there would be no sleep. As you do this exploration, you will become less and less attached to what you are not and much more aware of what you always already are.

You may also want to explore the following polarities:
- These thoughts belong to me–These thoughts belong to no one.
- Freedom is up to someone or something else–Freedom is up to "me."
- I am the body–I am infinite Beingness.

You may also want to explore the following question: "If I am not the body and I am not the mind, then what am I?"

The next seven pages of this book are designed to help further your own exploration. You can view them as your diary of progress during the week that you are working with this session. Use the space allowed on each page to write down your gains and realizations as they happen, as well as for notes on working with the various exercises.

# Day One

# Day Two

# Day Three

# Day Four

# Day Five

# Day Six

# Day Seven

"There is something far more beautiful than

nature–it is the Source of nature–

the ultimate beauty–God."

Lester Levenson

# Session 7

# The Self (Your Self)

This session is composed of aphorisms collected from various talks by Lester. Please allow yourself to ponder each one individually before going on to the next in order to get the maximum benefit.

- The Self, which is only your real Self, is the real "I" of you, knowing which, you know all there is to know.

- Knowing your Self is being your Self.

- The ultimate goal of every Being in the universe is total freedom, and that is when you are only your Self.

- The only reason why you are not aware of your Self is simply because you want to be only a single body in the world.

- Everyone will someday wake up to the fact that he is the Self.

- To see your Self, you have to quiet the mind enough. When the mind is being stimulated by the thousands of thoughts in the subconscious, there's little chance of seeing your Self. The thousands of thoughts culminate in tendencies. Drop a tendency and you eliminate the thousands of thoughts under it.

- The only things preventing you from being your Self are your mental habits, called tendencies or predispositions. Will them out!

- If you discover that the source of the tendencies or predispositions is the Self, your Self, you will drop them, then and there.

- When the mind gets free enough, then the Self of you takes over, and you are from then on Self-propelled.

- To be the non-Self requires much effort; it is the effort we feel in life.

- It requires no effort to be your Self!

- The effort that you think you use to try to be your Self is the effort you use in trying to resist being the non-Self ego.

- Your wishes to be the ego and, at the same time, not to be it, double the effort.

- All the effort you're involved in is the effort to be an ego, or to resist being an ego.

Do you see what the problem is? It is your constant effort. You must become effortless.

- There is only one real killing, and that's the killing of the Self. Kill the Self, and you've got ego and troubles. So everyone is a murderer of the Self who thinks he is an ego.

- The only reason why anyone isn't aware of the Self is because he wants other than that.

- If one wanted the Self as much as he wanted the world, he would soon have it.

- When you find more joy within yourself than in anything else, then you're really moving in the right direction. If you find any joy in life, you're in the wrong direction. Enjoying anything is wrong. Seek joy within. Be joy. There's nothing needed to enjoy if you are all-joyous. If we are enjoying anything, we are in duality.

  If I enjoy this, there's "I" and "this." If there's God (Self) alone, there can't be any "I" and "this." The basic truth is that you are all joy. Enjoying something will impose an extreme limitation upon your natural state of all-joy. To enjoy something, you're recognizing something other than you. So, I repeat, we should never enjoy anything. Seek joy only within, and then the natural state of infinite joy is discovered.

- There is really only one happiness: it is being our very own Self. The happier we are, the more we are dwelling in our Self.

- Every time you're high, you're only being your Self, and it feels terrific.

- Living in your Self is living in ecstasy. Living in worldly desires is living in misery.

- Everyone, in every moment, is experiencing his Self and, in every moment, saying otherwise.

- It's only without thought that you can be the Self.

- Discovering and being your Self is either easy or impossible.

- Finding the Self is the easiest thing in the universe when you do it. When you don't do it, when you continuously keep looking away from it, you can never see it. And then it is the most difficult thing in the universe.

- Being your Self is easy; being an ego is difficult.

- When you realize what you are, it's the dropping of what you are not that is the growth. Each time you see what you are, you should drop that which you are not.

- Everyone is seeking the Self, calling it by different names.

- Anyone who's seeking happiness is seeking the Self. There are two kinds of people in the world: those who are consciously seeking God, happiness, and the Self, and those who are unconsciously seeking them.

- In the consciousness of materiality (mammon), there is no God (Self).

- You cannot see God in the world until you see God in yourself.

- God is All and God is perfect. Therefore, anything that we see as imperfect is in us.

- If you see separation, you see not the Self.

- When the world is real, it is heavy. When the Self is real, the world is light.

- When our false identity as a body-mind disappears, our real identity as Self appears.

- We are the Self now. All that we have to do is to let go of the concept that we are not.

- The Self is God. The ego is the devil.

- God (your Self) is infinitely individual and individually infinite.

- The most beautiful beautiful is God.

- There is something far more beautiful than nature, it is the source of nature, the ultimate beauty–God.

- No matter how much trouble man can get himself into, God is more resourceful in getting him out of it.

- When we behave like God, we have God-like powers.

- God (Self) can materialize anything instantly.

- The All that is God is not every little thing; it is the singular same essence behind all the little things.

- God and good are sometimes used synonymously. Because everyone wants good, they make God good. God is above good and bad. However, good leads us to God.

- If God is All, that leaves no room for the devil.

- In reality, there is only God (your Self).

- It's better to think of Self rather than God, because you generally think of God as other than you, and you generally think of Self as you.

- There's no such thing as an external called God. There is a God, but it is the internal Beingness of each one.

- Everything that is, is the Self, has its isness, its Beingness, in your Self, in God.

- God is this world, the way this world is, and not the

apparency that we see.

- God–truth, the Self–is changeless. If God knew change, He wouldn't be changeless. There is no action in God. God knows nothing of this world as we see it. God is only the changeless Beingness behind the world.

- Everyone experiences his Self every moment of his life.

- Self is the nearest of the near and the dearest of the dear.

- Look to the Self for everything!

- If you want to get more comforts, know thy Self.

- The only answer to all problems is knowing your Self.

- We will never be completely satisfied until we are completely being the Self.

- To discover your Self is the reason why you came into this world.

- Everyone is seeking his Self in his every act. The ultimate happiness is the Self. Any other happiness is only a bit of the Self.

- When you know that the only joy there is is of the Self, you take it directly and, in its fullness, rather than meagerly, as you formerly took it.

- The only one needed to know your Self is yourself.

- This feeling of needing someone else to be your Self is ridiculous. It limits your being your Self.

- Everyone is actually the Self expressing the Self as extreme limitation, identifying as a limited body-mind. When you say "I" and add nothing to it, that's it.

- When you are not identifying with the ego, you are the Self.

- The only direct knowledge is of the Self. All other knowledge, needing something external to ourselves, is indirect.

- If, at this moment, you identify with your Self, you are infinite.

- That part of you that really is, your Beingness, is eternal. It's the I that you really are.

- The little self, the ego, is nothing but the innate, infinite Self assuming that it is limited. There are no two selves, one higher, the other lower; there are no two "I's." There is only one Self. It is perfect and always will be perfect, even though you make the false assumption that it is imperfect and limited. You are now, always were, and always will be your Self.

- Although one always experiences his Self, he usually needs to be directed to it before he becomes aware of it.

- It is the Self that is the source of the ego, the source of everything.

- You are every moment the unlimited Self, every moment saying, "I am limited." When you drop into the Self, you stop saying, "I am a limited body-mind." Look only at the Self; then the ego is eliminated.

- When you dwell in your Self, you have no desire to be liberated. It is only when you are in the ego that you desire liberation.

- The Self is not aware of the ego, and the ego is not aware of the Self.

- When I, the infinite Being, feel like a body, it's the infinite Being imagining it is feeling like a body.

- When the Self is real, the body is not real, and vice versa.

- Identify with your body, and the extreme limitations of a body are yours. Identify with your Self, and you are all things: all knowledge and power, with no limitations.

- There isn't anyone who couldn't materialize anything right now if he or she would just let go of identifying as the limited body.

- If you will discover your Self, you'll see that the body and mind are servant to you.

- Obtain and maintain direct experience of the Self. It is easier to obtain than to maintain direct experience.

- Every time you say "I," it's everything, it's all the power in the universe. Every time you add something to it, you pull it down into limitation.

- When you see the perfection, you see the other one as the other one really is, which is the real thing, the perfect Self.

- There's not a higher Self and a lower Self. There's only you identifying with your limitless Being or identifying with your limited being.

- You're never satisfied until you go all the way.

- There's only one thing that satisfies fully and eternally, and that's total awareness of your Self.

- Everyone is aware of a selfhood. It is the Self being wrongly identified as only a body.

- If you would just be aware only, you would be your Self. If you would be only, you would be your Self.

- This infinite glorious Being that we are, being absolutely perfect, can never change. It's always there.

- The greatest of all teachers is your Self.

- Look to your Self until you see it completely.

- All Beingness is God, your Self.

- In the Self, there is no haver, having or thing had. There is no doer, doing or thing done. There's no knower, knowing or thing known. There is only Being, being all Beingness.

- When man seeks and discovers the seeker, he discovers that:
  In the Self:
  God is not being something, God is Beingness.
  God is not conscious of anything, God is consciousness.
  God does not enjoy anything, God is joy.
  God does not love anything or anyone, God is love.

  In man:
  His Beingness is God.
  His consciousness is God.
  His joy is God
  His love is God.

- Act as though you are the Self. This will lead you to seeing it.

- The reality of you (Self) is perfect: all joyous, all glorious, all happy.

- The higher you go, the more you realize your Self, and the more you treat others as your own Self.

- Being the Self is being selfless. In that state, you are interested only in serving others, in serving them as your Self.

- The Self is absolute, profound, indescribable peace.

- The only requisite for the realization of the Self, your Self, is stillness.

- When one realizes his Self, all his actions and possessions are not perceived as his. He has given up "me" and "mine." Everything is the Self.

- When you experience the Self, you can't tell about it. Anything you can tell something about isn't it. It's the state of only being. There's no action there, there's no form there. It's isness, and that's all that it is. You can't use it, you can't know it, you can only be it. When you're there, there's only one, only you, and that's all there is.

- Anything but the Self is wholly imagination. The ego is only an apparent actor in the imaginary story script you wrote. Thou art that, here and now. Do not delude yourself. Drop your illusory limitation.

- The Self is quiescence: perfect awareness with perfect stillness. He who seeks God will not find God in duality. There is no human, since God is All. There is no time, no becoming. There is no creating in total perfection.

Only God beholds God, there being nothing else.
Only God loves God, God being All.
Be still and know that you are God!

- There is only God, nothing else. If there is only God, then I
  am that. At the end of the road, we discover that there is only
  "I," all alone.

- You are the Self, saying otherwise, but that doesn't make it
  so. No matter how much you say otherwise, you are that
  infinite Being right now.

- You can't become your Self, you already are!

- Every time you say "I," that's the Self–if you would only
  stop there!

- The word "I," with nothing added to it, is your Self. When
  you just say "I," that feeling of "I" is the Self. When you say "I
  am something," that isn't it, but just pure "I" and only "I" is it.
  When that is all you see and all you know, that's God, your
  Self. That's why God is closer than flesh! Just hold onto the
  word "I," only, "I, I, I, I." Try it when you are alone. Just "I, I"
  and not "I am a body," but "I, I, I, I"–that feeling of being.
  Hold that; experience it. Be it! It is your Godhead–your Self!

## Comments:

To summarize: There is no growing into the ultimate Being that you are. It is you right now and has always been. Every moment you are choosing to either identify with your limitless Beingness or with the limited you.

Choose now to be still and know what you are.

## Suggestions for the week:

Allow yourself to explore the "I" meditation that Lester described above. Simply repeat the word "I" to yourself without adding anything to it. As you do, allow yourself to drop everything but the "I" as best you can, and rest as the feeling or the presence that you are aware of as you repeat the word. Allow yourself to feel into that presence more and more as you repeat "I," until that is all there is. Then, just rest as that which you have always been.

You can do this meditation in isolation or in action. Either way you will be supporting yourself to rediscover your true nature and make it a conscious part of your awareness in every moment.

You may also want to explore the following polarities:

- Could I allow the world to appear as heavy as it does? – Could I allow it to be as light as it is?
- Could I allow there to appear to be as much effort as there is? –Could I allow there to be as much effortlessness as there is?
- Could I allow myself to be as identified with the body-mind as I am? –Could I allow myself to be as identified as the Self as I am?
- I am–I.

The next seven pages of this book are designed to help further your own exploration. You can view them as your diary of progress during the week that you are working with this session. Use the space allowed on each page to write down your gains and realizations as they happen, as well as for notes on working with the various exercises.

# Day One

# Day Two

# Day Three

_____

# Day Four

# Day Five

# Day Six

# Day Seven

# The Next Steps

Congratulations on completing Book 5 of *Happiness Is Free*. As you apply what you have learned to your quest for the ultimate happiness, you should find your apparent problems dropping away and your natural freedom shining forth. This will continue until you are at rest in every moment as the Beingness that you have always been and you see the exquisite perfection of All That Is.

The following suggestions are designed to help you get the maximum benefit from the material in this book on an ongoing basis:

1. Allow yourself to use the material in every part of your life. If you only thought about and explored freedom for a few minutes a day, you would gain tremendous benefits. However, if you allowed freedom to be in your mind and heart throughout the day, those results would increase exponentially. Like everything else, the more energy you put into the process, the more you get out of it.

2. Review the material often. Every time you reread and work with the ideas in this book, you will get more out of them. As you mature spiritually, you will understand and be able to apply what you learn on deeper levels. Treat each review as though it were your first time. Explore all the exercises, and allow a full week for each session.

3. Share what you have learned. Communicating these ideas and practices with your friends, relatives, and acquaintances should stretch you and deepen your own understanding. Additional benefits come from surrounding yourself with like-minded people who are also interested in deepening their freedom. However, please remember only to share this material with those who are truly interested in hearing about it. Grant those you know their Beingness—see them as already perfect—whether or not they share your interest.

4. Start or join a *Happiness Is Free* support group. An energetic lift comes "when two or more are gathered in thy name." The larger the group, the more this energetic lift is magnified. Lester used to say that the energy in groups is "squared." In other words, two people have the power of two times two, three people have the power of three times three, and so on. Another benefit of participating in a group is seeing the material from perspectives other than your own. This can deepen your understanding. (See p. 212, Guidelines for *Happiness Is Free* Support Groups.)

5. Read the other four books in this series. Together they comprise a total of thirty-five sessions. Each book, in and of itself, is a complete course on the ultimate happiness. But if you have enjoyed reading and working with this one, you would probably enjoy and benefit from the other books as well.

6. Learn the Sedona Method®. As we have already mentioned, Lester's material truly comes alive when it is combined with the Sedona Method®. Lester was so excited about this part of his teaching that he devoted the last twenty years of his life to perfecting and promoting it. There are two great ways to learn the Sedona Method®. You can explore the power of letting go through live seminars, which are offered worldwide, or in audiotape programs.

To get information on the Sedona Method® Course, you may visit the Sedona Training Associates website: **www.sedona.com**, e-mail us at **release@sedona.com**, or call us at **(928) 282-3522**. At the end of this book there is a fill-out form that you can also use to request further information.

7. Review and deepen your use of Holistic Releasing™. The Holistic Releasing™ process is an integral part of this book. If you have enjoyed working with the polarities at the end of the sessions, you would probably also enjoy our tape programs *Practical Freedom* and *Absolute Freedom* or attending a seminar on this technique. (See the contact information above.)

**You are the key to your own happiness. All you need to do is use that key to unlock the secrets of freedom and happiness that are waiting to be discovered right within your own heart. Good luck and enjoy.**

# Guidelines for *Happiness Is Free* Support Groups

The goal of a group should be to support each participant in gaining the most they can from their use of the material. It is important that a safe space be created so that everyone feels free to participate, yet never feels pressured to do so. This is best facilitated if a different member of the group is given an opportunity to be the leader each time the group meets, if they chose to do so. It helps to prevent one person from dominating the group. It also allows participants to stretch in the direction of helping others.

If anyone brings up an emotional or physical issue that would usually be handled by a trained medical professional, they should be encouraged to seek a health professional. These support groups should never be used as a substitute for competent medical attention. They should be used as an aid to each participant's personal and spiritual growth.

It is helpful to have the support group meet once a week since each session is designed to be used for a full week. If at first that is difficult, meeting once a month would still be helpful.

If you are using private residences for your meetings, it is also helpful to rotate the location where the support group is being held so that the burden for hosting is not borne by only one person. However, if you can find a centrally located free public location we encourage you to use it on an ongoing basis.

The following instructions are for the leader of the support group.

## Welcome Everyone

Start with a brief quote from Lester from the week's session. Then allow for a few minutes of silence to give everyone an opportunity to ponder the quote and to get centered and present in the room. Do your best to create the safe space for everyone attending.

## Ice Breaker

Have the group share their names and a gain that they have experienced so far from *Happiness Is Free*.

## Partner Work

Have each person in the group find a partner and support each other in doing an exercise from the week's session. Select an exercise that would be appropriate to do with a partner from the book. Spend approximately thirty minutes on the exercise, either having the partners switch back and forth, taking turns facilitating each other, or time it so each participant has about fifteen minutes to do their exploration with the support of their partner.

Have each partner open their copy of *Happiness Is Free* to the exercise being explored, so they can remember the verbiage and remind each other to change the wording to the third person using the pronoun "you" instead of "I."

### Read the Following Statement Aloud

Be there with and for your partner as best you can. Grant them their Beingness by allowing them to have their own exploration. When you are asking your partner to let go, do your best to let go as you facilitate your partners in releasing. You will find that this happens naturally if you are open to it. Refrain from leading, judging their responses, or giving them advice. Also refrain from discussing the explorations until you have both completed them and you have spent a few minutes in silence. Be sure to validate your partner's point of view, even if it does not agree with your own.

Please refrain from playing the role of counselor or therapist even if you're a trained counselor or therapist. If your partner brings up a medical condition that would ordinarily require a trained medical professional, recommend that they get whatever support they need in this area. If you are not sure whether or not they truly need medical support, you can recommend that they seek professional medical attention, just to be sure.

### Have Group Share

Have volunteers from the group share what they got from the exercise. Make sure the group validates their perspective, and support them in letting go and moving up into greater freedom.

### Sharing Gains

Give the group another opportunity to share gains if they choose.

### Silence

Have the group spend a few minutes allowing their beingness to be in silence.

## Thank Everyone for Coming

Thank everyone for coming and encourage the group to maintain the silence within as they go home or go about their day.

# Gains from *Happiness is Free:*
## Book 5

Please use the space on this page and the next to share your gains from working with this material. If you would prefer you can use a separate sheet of paper or e-mail us at **release@sedona.com** to send us your gains.

## Gains from book 5 *continued*

_____

_____

_____

_____

_____

_____

_____

_____

_____

_____

_____

_____

I give Sedona Training Associates permission to quote my comments in promotional materials and future books. I understand that in exchange I am entitled to receive a discount on the Sedona Method® Course or the Holistic Releasing™ tape sets.

Signature

Name

Address

City, State                                        Zip or Postal Code

Phone

E-mail Address

# WE ARE HERE FOR YOU

Sedona Training Associates is dedicated to helping you liberate your true nature and to have, be, and do all that you choose. Our products have been created for this purpose. To accelerate your progress, we highly encourage you to attend one of our live seminars or purchase a tape program. The following are some of our offerings.

## The Sedona Method® Course,

both as a live seminar or as our home study audio program, will show you how to elegantly and easily tap your natural ability to let go of any unwanted thought or feeling on the spot. In addition to gaining deeper awareness of the ultimate truth and your natural state of unlimited happiness, the Sedona Method® can free you to have any or all of the following: more money, better relationships, more radiant health and well being, more effective goal achievement, plus how to break bad habits and other self-sabotaging behaviors, lose weight, stop smoking, and sleep better.

You will also be able to easily, effortlessly and joyously free yourself from stress, tension, panic, fear, anxiety, depression, indecision, low self-esteem and self-doubt, fatigue, insomnia, codependency, uncontrolled anger, and grief. In short, you will enjoy living a happier, more productive, more satisfying, more loving and happy life.

The Holistic Releasing™ process, as you have probably already experienced from reading this book, can also accomplish all of the above. It is an integral part of our advanced seminars. You can also deepen your experience of this powerful tool by exploring our Holistic Releasing™ tape programs *Absolute Freedom* and *Practical Freedom.*

**Absolute Freedom:** This audio set utilizes Holistic Releasing™ to help you to easily recognize and dissolve the barriers that you imagine are keeping you from perceiving your true nature. These recordings will help you to discover the natural state of Beingness that has always been available to you here and now. You will discover that who you are has only appeared to be hidden by your self-imposed sense of limitation. You have always been absolutely free.

**Practical Freedom:** This audio set is designed to help you to rediscover the freedom to have, be, or do whatever you choose as an alive and practical part of your everyday life. It will help free you to perform at your best in every situation, and live your life with greater ease and clarity. As you apply Holistic Releasing™, you will find that even long-standing challenges dissolve and are replaced by a greater sense of mastery.

# Book and Information Order Form

Please send me free information on the
Sedona Method® Course. ❏

Please send me free information on the
*Practical Freedom* and *Absolute Freedom*
Holistic Releasing™ tape sets. ❏

I have enclosed my signed gains sheet from
the page before to get a discount. ❏

I choose not to send gains at this time.
Please just send me the information. ❏

| Quantity | Item | Amount | Total |
|---|---|---|---|
| | Happiness Is Free: Book 1 | $24.95 USD | |
| | Happiness Is Free: Book 2 | $24.95 USD | |
| | Happiness Is Free: Book 3 | $24.95 USD | |
| | Happiness Is Free: Book 4 | $24.95 USD | |
| | Happiness Is Free: Book 5 | $24.95 USD | |
| | | Shipping | |
| | (AZ Residents only please include 9.30 % sales tax) **Tax** | | |
| | | **Total** | |

Shipping in USA and Canada $4.95 USD per book,
and $9.95 USD per book worldwide.

(Please continue your details overleaf)

## Please Print Clearly

Name

Address

City                        State                        Zip

Phone *(Home)*                        *(Office)*

E-mail Address

**VISA**  **MasterCard**  **AMERICAN EXPRESS**  **DISCOVER** NOVUS

Visa Master Card American Express Discover

Credit Card # ☐☐☐☐  ☐☐☐☐  ☐☐☐☐  ☐☐☐☐

Expiration ☐☐ / ☐☐

I authorize you to charge my card for the above amount ☐

Signature

Make checks payable and mail orders to:
**Sedona Training Associates**
60 Tortilla Dr. Sedona, AZ 86336
928-282-3522, 888-282-5656
www.sedona.com